You Are My Sunshine
The Jimmie Davis Story

You Are My Sunshine
The Jimmie Davis Story

An Affectionate Biography

by

Gus Weill

PELICAN PUBLISHING COMPANY
Gretna 1995

First printing, February 1977
Second printing, June 1977
First Pelican printing, June 1987
Fourth printing, September 1991
Fifth printing, January 1995

Library of Congress Cataloging-in-Publication Data

Weill, Gus.
    You are my sunshine.

    Reprint. Originally published: Waco, Tex.: Word
Books, © 1977.
    1. Davis, Jimmie, 1902-   . 2. Country
musicians--United States--Biography. I. Title
[ML420.D315W4   1987]   784.5'2'00924   [B]   87-11898
ISBN: 0-88289-660-1 (pbk.)

Manufactured in the United States of America
Published by Pelican Publishing Company, Inc.
1101 Monroe Street, Gretna, Louisiana 70053

This book is dedicated to the people of Louisiana, who have been very kind to a sharecropper from Beech Springs.

Contents

"*I have wined and dined with the swankiest of the swank and broken bread with the poorest of the poor, but come what may, they can't ration anything I haven't done without.*"

—Jimmie Davis

Acknowledgments

No book of this kind can possibly be the product of one or two people. Close to one hundred and twenty interviews were conducted over a year's time. It is impossible to list everyone who so willingly helped, some by the painful reliving of the past that was not always kind. The following people were of particular help:

Ed Reed of Baton Rouge, who conducted all of the brilliant research into the Davis family background; the Honorable Chris Faser; the Honorable William J. Dodd; the Honorable Rolfe McCollister; Dr. Robert G. Lee; Governor Sam Houston Jones; Charles East, Jr., our editor; Mary H. Alston, our typist; and last but certainly not least, a couple of ladies who laughed and cried with us, Anna Davis and Ann Weill.

From the subject and the author, thank you.

From the Author

This is not a critical biography. That will have to come later when all the participants have left the stage they once occupied so furiously and with so much passion.

I hope that this book will entertain, be somewhat informational, and, above all else, be greatly inspirational to all who start life way back of the crowd, miles and miles from even the starting mark, as did the book's subject, Jimmie H. Davis.

That Jimmie survived at all is a kind of miracle. That he did so many things so well is unquestionably just that: a miracle.

There are three Jimmie Davises in this book as will become immediately obvious. There's the Jimmie Davis who has a master's degree, who's traveled all over the world, and who has been on an intimate basis with many men who led this world.

There's the Jimmie Davis who has succeeded at everything he has ever done. He's been governor of his state twice. He's a member of the Country Music Hall of Fame and the Song Writers Hall of Fame. He's been named Gospel Singer of the Year.

Then there's the Jimmie Davis who quietly mounts the stage and can make any audience laugh or cry, depending on just what he wants to do. That's a different Jimmie Davis—a rural one, murdering the English language, right off someone else's farm, eyes open in shock, mouth open in astonishment at such curious inventions as electricity and even plumbing.

After working with Jimmie all these months, the author has come away with a dominant impression. A lot of people talk about humility. Jimmie H. Davis really has it.

Gus Weill
May, 1976
Baton Rouge, Louisiana

Introduction

It doesn't matter who you are or where you are. It doesn't matter whether you're the poorest black man in some eastern ghetto or a redneck freezing in a share-cropper's cabin; the story of Jimmie Davis can be your story. It's more than the story of one man, more than a story of triumph over all the odds. It's the story of faith in a nation and belief in God and what happened to one man who possessed both in abundance.

Chances are you won't go from a shotgun shack to the Governor's Mansion of your state twice. Chances are you won't become a world-renowned artist and composer of perhaps the most popular song ever written, *You Are My Sunshine*. But the chances are that if you'll believe, if you'll have faith, if you'll work with all your heart and might, if you'll love your fellow man and hope that he loves you, no man, no thing, no system, no minus sign will ever stop you. Troubles may delay you for a while and you may even stumble off the road you meant to take, but you won't be stopped.

You'll have the secret ingredient to which Jimmie Davis attributes most of his amazing success. You'll have a piece of the American Dream. What you do with it is of course up to you. When a man loses faith in it, it can become a nightmare. But if a man is willing, willing to dream it, willing to sacrifice for it, he'll own the dream. It will be his forever.

That's what Jimmie Davis' story is really about: The American Dream.

1. *One Spring Day*

They lived two and one-half miles out of Beech Springs, a community in North Louisiana, in a three-room cabin that belonged to someone else. The owner's name was W. R. Guess, and they farmed his land, too—"all that two mules could work."

There were eleven children and their parents plus Grandpa and Grandma Davis living in the two rooms and a kitchen.

A sister, Elsie, aged four, became ill and they treated her as best they could with simple home remedies. There were no doctors for miles about, and even if there had been there was no money to pay a doctor.

The law of survival was simple, and though they never spoke of it they all knew it: if you were sick, you got well or you died.

It became obvious to all that Elsie was dwindling away, and in a short time her sight went. They discovered this by moving a candle back and forth in front of her face. She didn't see it.

One spring morning at about nine, Jimmie Davis and some of his brothers and sisters were playing outside. Their father stepped out of the cabin and said, "Youall better come on in. Elsie's dying."

They gathered about the child's bed. Her tiny fist held tightly to her mother's, and her sightless eyes looked straight ahead. Then the child began to sing.

> School days, school days,
> Dear old golden rule days.

The song stopped, the tiny hand let go, the blind eyes closed. Elsie Davis had lost the cruel game of survival.

Papa said, "Jimmie, you help me," and the family went quietly about the business of preparing one of its own for her Maker.

Mrs. Davis sewed lace about the collar of Elsie's one good dress, and she sewed lace about a small pillow on which they would lay Elsie's head. Jimmie and his father got some rough lumber planks and pulled some nails out of an old picket fence, and they built a box for Elsie.

Mrs. Davis made a tiny bed within the box and put the pillow in. Then the mother bathed her daughter and combed her hair. Some of the Davis children were sent to neighboring farms to notify friends. Jimmie and some of the kids went to the Antioch Church Cemetery to help dig a grave.

The Davises, the rest of their children, and Elsie were aboard the wagon for the silent ride to the grave. When they got there, joined now by four or five other wagons, they sang *Amazing Grace* and *How Firm a Foundation*. A neighbor read some Scripture and said a few words.

2

Strangely he spoke about hope and not about poverty or even about despair.

Then, with ropes, the box containing Elsie was lowered into red clay earth. The grave was covered. There was a closing prayer; then all got back onto the wagons and headed home.

Mrs. Davis told her family, "I don't think youall ought to play for a day or two," and for that period of time the family sat about in silence wishing they had a way to express how they felt.

That was as long as they could formally mourn. There were fields to be plowed, mouths to be fed. It was time to get back to their main task of making it still another day.

2. The Long Journey

to Another Man's Land

Where did they come from, these desperate people locked to a land that was not theirs?

The answer lies in a bitter and long-ago yesterday.

In 1839 on a farm near Cuthbert, Georgia, a ten-year-old boy named Henry Davis took a final look at the piece of ground he called home and had helped to cultivate since he was old enough to walk, and began a journey on foot.

The journey was to be some six hundred miles across the foothills of the Blue Ridge and Appalachian Mountains, through the evergreen-carpeted terrain of central Alabama and Mississippi, down into the Yazoo Basin and across the two-mile-wide Mississippi River, and finally into the red clay hills of southwestern Arkansas.

It was a remarkable journey for a ten-year-old who had never been more than a few miles from a sharecropper's cabin.

Still, what he did was not all that unusual. "Walking away from home" was a common phenomenon in the pre-Civil War South. "Walking away from home" meant one less mouth to feed, a little more living room, and hopefully, because no one really knew, perhaps it meant something better. It was the kind of necessity and challenge that caused this land we call the United States to be settled in the first place.

Henry Davis began his trip with two distinctions: his extreme youth and a beautiful tenor voice. Even as a youngster, he was said to delight young and old alike with folk and religious songs.

His journey finally ceased in a small valley west of Camden, Arkansas, in the extreme western part of the state. It was almost a duplicate of the land he had left, with one exception: it was less populated. There was never any doubt about what young Henry Davis would do for a livelihood—the only thing he knew anything about, farming.

He found employment on a farm of a Mr. Kesterson and soon became not only a valued employee but a valued member of the family. He later courted and wed Kesterson's daughter, Jemima Elizabeth, nine years his junior. Between the period of 1854 and 1864, the couple begat six children.

In 1863 Henry was forced to leave his family as he donned Confederate gray to fight in the Civil War. Following the ending of that war in 1865, it was three years before Arkansas was readmitted to the Union and Henry Davis returned home. From then until 1875, he sired four more children, for a total of ten by the time he had reached his middle 40s!

By the year 1883, Henry was an established farmer on the Kesterson holdings in Arkansas. Of the ten children, four had grown to maturity, left home, and begun to raise families on their own.

With the possible exception that he was working someone else's land, he had no reason to leave Arkansas. But his journey was not over yet.

A son, Henry Cicero Davis, drowned in a stream nearby where his father was shaving. Naked to the waist, Henry plunged into the stream and in a moment surfaced with his son's body. Cicero never regained consciousness and Henry Davis was never to be the same. He never shaved again, and in later years the long gray beard was to be his constant reminder of the death of his child who bore his name.

Shortly after this tragedy, Henry received a letter from a nephew, James Lucius Durham, the son of J. L. Durham and Henry's sister Eliza. The elder Durhams had left Randolph County, Georgia, in 1859, taking with them their family of eleven and settling in Louisiana. Among them was Henry's nephew James, who became an affluent landowner.

James Durham had never forgotten his young uncle Henry, especially that good tenor voice.

"Dear Uncle," James wrote, "I have more land than I need and am willing to deed you forty acres free, if you will move down here, just to hear you sing again some old time Georgia songs."

Three months after receiving this letter, Henry Davis arrived in Louisiana.

His arrival created much excitement, and the family reminisced until midnight. The following morning, James took his uncle for a tour of his holdings and reiterated his offer to exchange a farm for a song.

Henry confessed to his nephew that James' sister Sallie, who lived in nearby Marthaville, Louisiana, in adjoining

Natchitoches Parish to the west, had also written him, suggesting that he would be better off buying land to the west than accepting James' offer of free land.

Finally, Henry settled in Sabine Parish, not far from Marthaville, where he farmed as a tenant. He stayed there four years, then moved to Calcasieu Parish to the south, staying two years as a tenant. By this time he had put aside enough money to rent a farm, and he moved to a spot near James' farm in Atlanta in Winn Parish.

The combination of frequent relocations and the rigors of farm life made it difficult to obtain an education, and Henry's youngest son, Sam Jones Davis, was by now nineteen years old and had received a total of two months' formal education. In all probability that wouldn't have bothered young Jones Davis, except that he fell in love with a well-fixed man's daughter, Sara Elizabeth Works, whose father Jessie owned a sawmill between Sabine and Calcasieu Parishes.

The Works family did not look favorably upon the uneducated young farmer who wanted to marry their daughter.

Jones Davis arranged with his father to be responsible for the cultivation of the farm himself if his father agreed to allow him to attend school. On New Years Day in 1893, nineteen-year-old Jones Davis enrolled in a one-room schoolhouse two miles east of Atlanta, Louisiana.

His teacher was to be his second cousin, John Pickney Durham, son of James Durham, who had offered Henry Davis a farm in exchange for a song.

In his memoirs John Pickney tells us that Jones was tutored at recess so that he could enter the third grade with larger pupils rather than begin in first grade with youngsters young enough to be his own children.

With a bit of education, Jones began in earnest to court Sara Elizabeth Works.

Jessie Works was adamant, his daughter could not marry Jones Davis!

Jones and Sara could not accept this. They simply loved each other too much. On January 17, 1897, at the age of nineteen, Sara was married to Jones. She was warmly welcomed by the Davises, but her father never forgave her, and there was no further contact between father and daughter for the rest of their lives.

Jones and Sara lived for a short time in Rapides Parish, outside the city of Alexandria, Louisiana. But the attraction of the land was too much for Jones, and he moved his family to the tiny community of Beech Springs, which at that time contained several dozen families, all of them farming.

Jones Davis owned no land and being without resources was unable to buy any. W. R. Guess, who owned the general store in nearby Quitman, owned more land around Beech Springs than he could farm, so Jones took to sharecropping or "farming on halves" for him.

This arrangement meant that Jones Davis would provide the labor while Guess provided the seed, fertilizer, the mule, the plow, and the land, and they would split whatever revenue the cotton yield would be.

Jones Davis was to be a tenant farmer for twenty-five years before he was able, with the help of the Federal Land Bank, to make a down payment on a farm of his own. During those twenty-five years there was one occasion, a single year, when the family did not go into debt. It was to be a hard, bitter struggle.

Jones Davis summed it up years later: "Make a living, mister? We didn't try to make anything. We just tried to survive."

A man was pretty much alone except for his faith, his family, and a few neighbors. And there were good neighbors about Beech Springs: Andersons, Baileys, Barnards, Blalocks, Bradleys, Carsons, Driscolls, Ducks, Fergusons, Grissoms, Harveys, Hargroves, Koonces, McCravys, Peels, Pirkles, Rasburys, Shows, Strouds, Suttons, Thompsons, Thorntons, Walsworths, Watsons, Wigleys and Womacks, among others.

One of Jones' eleven children was Jimmie Houston Davis.

When was Jimmie Davis born? He says he remembers that it was during cotton-picking time. "We lost all track of time," Davis says and tells this story to illustrate.

"One Sunday morning we all got in the wagon and drove four miles to a neighboring friend's farm to spend the day. When we got there, they were all in the field picking cotton. They told us it was Tuesday, but as long as we'd come that great distance it might as well be Sunday. They came in from the field, washed up, and put on their Sunday clothes. We had the Sabbath on a Tuesday."

3. *Early Childhood*

Jimmie Davis' very first memory was probably like the earliest memory of a lot of children: a certain Christmas. But what a Christmas! On Christmas morning there were palm prints (made with wet hands) on the black-smoked chimney, sure proof that Santa had been by the night before!

"We didn't get much as I recall," says Jimmie, "an apple, an orange and a big stick of candy. But that was enough because we didn't know how little we really had compared to just about everyone else. We thought people were supposed to starve most of the time and go about half naked."

He next remembers a "great trip that the family took." The Davises hitched up the mules to the wagon, and all got aboard—including little Jimmie, then aged five—and went the great distance of five miles to Quitman, where they planned to spend the night with relatives.

The relatives lived in a tent, the father worked in the lumber mill. Jimmie recalls that his relative's oldest daughter was sent with a bucket to borrow some flour from a neighbor for biscuits, when it started raining and then hailing. His cousin put the bucket over her head to protect it from the elements and it got hung there. And he remembers her running and falling, the bucket hanging on her head so she could not see where she was going nor how to get out of the ditches half full of water.

The tent blew down and collapsed on the whole family, and when the rain had finally stopped, the Davises knew that a place as big as Quitman was far too dangerous for them. Besides, they were worried about the cattle back on the farm at home. After they had dried themselves by a potbellied stove, neighbors gave them clothes to wear home. Davis' father, a man about 6–2, was given a suit that might fit a man 5–1, and Jimmie recalls that he was dressed in someone's nightgown for the wagon ride home. "We got home about midnight, rounded up the livestock, washed in a big tub, and put Cloverine Salve on all our bruises; then we went to bed. We saw our relatives about a month later and the tent was back up. I gathered they were waiting for the next storm."

Jimmie went to work at age five. His family was sharecropping for Jim Harvey, who offered young Davis his first job: hoeing cotton. There's no way he'll ever forget that job. Harvey owned a jackass, an animal Davis had never seen before. "It looked like a kind of peculiar mule, and when he began to bray, it scared the life out of me. I ran and tried to jump over a barbed-wire fence, a tall one, and almost made it."

The proof of that encounter with jackass and fence remains on Jimmie's right shin today—a three-inch scar that he recalls they treated with turpentine from a pine tree and wrapped with a piece of bed sheet. After first aid, it was cotton-hoeing time.

"I worked a couple of hours, and Mr. Harvey held out a quarter in one hand, a nickel in the other and told me to take my choice. I knew the difference but I didn't want to take advantage, so I took the nickel. It looked as big as a silver dollar to me."

By the following year Davis' family had moved into town, where his father was a section hand for the Rock Island Line for a dollar a day. Davis recalls, "Two or three years later, he had worked himself up to a dollar and a dime. A man named Richard Moore who owned a farm out of town hired me to cut bushes. I went in for lunch but it was only 8:30. I went in again but it was just 10:00 A.M. I never saw anything take so long to come as noon and lunch."

Jimmie recalls one dismal and dangerous experience. "I had sore eyes, most of us did; there was simply no hygiene at all. I was six. My eyes began to hurt terribly during the night, and my mother got up by a kerosene lamp and put something in my eyes to soothe me. Then it really began to hurt. I can remember my father's frightened voice coming up out of the darkness and telling my mother to check what she had put in my eyes. She did, and I heard her scream. She had filled my eyes with turpentine. She went into the kitchen and got some cow's cream—cream from an old bob-tailed cow named Lil. We kept the cream in my eyes until breakfast, then it was back to cutting bushes."

At about that time Jimmie's memory of church begins. He can recall getting sleepy and his mother stretching him out on the bench from which "I fell off and sprained my thumb. I whooped and hollered."

Here he recalls his first hymn, *Amazing Grace.*

There were different churches in those early years as the Davises moved back and forth from town to country trying to eke out an existence. In Beech Springs it was the Solemn Thought Baptist Church.

What about those early preachers? Let Davis tell it.

> The wife of a cousin of mine, A. P. "Apple Pie" Durham, taught him to read and write after they were married, and he became a preacher. No telling how many people Apple Pie baptized. He was a fine, entertaining speaker, a man who studied Scripture and did amazingly well with a very limited education.
>
> One Sunday he stopped at a house near the church to freshen up, sprinkle himself with Hoyt's Cologne. After liberally dousing himself in the stuff, he shoved the bottle down into a back pocket. He got to church and commenced to preach. Suddenly he stopped, got pale and then snow white as the sweat poured from his face. He fell to the floor with his face in his hands, groaning. The deacons rushed up and asked him what was wrong. "I'm bleeding to death," he told them. See, the bottle of Hoyt's Cologne had broken in his pocket, and he thought that the wetness pouring down his leg was blood. There was no more preaching that day.

When *did* the day begin for the Davis family? When they could see, which was usually about 4:00 A.M. First there was breakfast, consisting of biscuits, syrup, butter, bacon, and lots of flour gravy. Then to work—plowing, hoeing, picking cotton—with always at least one baby riding on the cotton sack.

Mama left the field a little earlier than the others to prepare lunch, which could consist of cornbread, peas, greens, maybe a rabbit or a squirrel, and, on special occasions, a potato pie.

14

At 1:00 P.M. it was back into the field until darkness. Supper was like lunch. "We never had indigestion. Fourteen hours' work a day in a field seems to have cured just about everything."

After supper the family washed their feet in a big tub. Saturday was the day for a full bath, with the washtub filled with warm water out in the yard. "The first one in the tub got a good bath, but the last one got a mud bath!"

The Davises finished the day off with a brief Scripture reading by the father. "Papa wanted us to remember the Bible, but the Scripture had to be brief because we were so exhausted and 4:00 A.M. and another day wasn't that far away."

Where'd the eleven Davis children and mother and father sleep? Those who could, got into a bed; the rest slept on pallets.

Saturday was the same as the weekdays, except on Saturday night they got together at someone's house to sing "and have a candy pulling."

"You put butter or grease on your hands and commenced stringing the taffy out until you had candy. Usually you had a boy and a girl on either end of the pulling. I guess that was one of the earliest forms of courting. No telling how many marriages got started at a candy pulling."

On Sunday, necks and ears were carefully washed for church; then a pair of small mules was hitched up to the wagon. Mules were highly significant to Davis for a very special reason.

"The mules, like everything else we used, belonged to someone else, and all my life I wanted to plow with mules that were mine. Right after I was elected Governor, I bought a mule and took it with all the rigging

15

to my farm near Newellton. There I turned over the earth with my own mule. I can't recall anything giving me that kind of pleasure as getting that garden ready for planting with my own mule."

After church, Sunday was a big day for visiting or having visitors. Davis remembers once when there were forty guests for Sunday dinner. "Mama put more water in the gravy, killed more chickens, put on more peas. The kids had to wait; there wasn't enough room at the tables set up outside. People shared them. No one had anything; most of us were sharecroppers."

What about school? Well, it was take it or leave it, with no law of compulsory attendance. In addition you had to buy your own books. Some went, some didn't. "We all went because my parents insisted. Right from the start, I hated to see the school day end because I knew that cotton was waiting."

Jimmie's first school was in Quitman in a Mrs. Wilder's home. "From the very first day I decided to behave, when I saw Mrs. Wilder whip her son with a buggy whip for eating her lunch. Seeing that made a better child of me!"

Jimmie liked spelling best. They had a book or two but mostly used a slate. There were cedar pencils (five for a nickel). At recess they played a game called Town Ball, which was a kind of baseball.

Each student brought his lunch in a little bucket, and lunch could consist of a piece of meat in the middle of a biscuit, sandwich-like, or a specialty made by punching a hole in a biscuit with your finger, then filling it with syrup.

Jimmie recalls getting into trouble in the third grade. By then he was in a three-room school in Quitman. "The very first morning, our teacher, Miss Lena Allgood, was writing on the blackboard when I spotted a big long corn-

16

cob on the floor. I picked it up, and someone suggested that I throw it at the blackboard. All my classmates assured me they wouldn't tell who had done it. They crossed their hearts. Well, I threw it, and it broke into three pieces. Miss Allgood turned around and asked, 'Who did that?' The entire class, sounding like a well-rehearsed chorus, replied loudly, 'Jimmie Davis!' Miss Allgood said, 'Come up here, Jimmie.' She sat me on her lap and made me sit there like a baby for the rest of the day. I felt like a fool, and that's the last corncob I ever threw! This also taught me to be careful who you trust."

The class did a lot of singing, mostly Stephen C. Foster songs. Every Friday afternoon there was what they called "Friday Afternoon Society," which was really a talent show. Jimmie Davis sang.

He recalls a farmer named Del Grissom "because he had a beautiful tenor voice and because he was the very first person who told me my singing wasn't all that bad and maybe I ought to sing some more."

Those were the days of a lot of itinerant preachers—men going from house to house, town to town, spreading the gospel. About once a month, one would spend the night with the Davis family.

"After supper the preacher would read the Scriptures and make a short talk, then close with a prayer. If Papa had a few nickels, he'd give them to him. But mostly we gave preachers potatoes, a fryer, two or three buckets of syrup. Sometimes a family would plant an acre for the preacher. Whatever grew on it was his. Honestly, those were extremely dedicated man, just barely keeping body and soul together. They had faith, though, and a respect grew in me for men who could give so much to other men and ask so little."

Preachers were an important way to get the news, as

were drummers coming through town. There was no radio, and no one really knew what was going on in the nation, much less the world.

The Davis family did subscribe to one magazine, *Comfort*. It was full of weather predictions and advice to lovers. They bought a magazine called the *Ladies Birthday Almanac*. It told them when to plant and when to operate on or castrate the animals. Most of the counsel was based on the moon, and Davis promises that some day soon he's going to grow a crop based on just that!

Was childhood happy?

"I didn't know anything, and it seemed that every day I was learning something. It was very happy."

4. *Growing Up*

Just how was it to be growing up as one of eleven children? Jimmie Davis' answer tells a lot about the man himself.

"It was one great, continuous party. We enjoyed each other because we had something going on all of the time. It's great to be a part of a big family. The companionship is beautiful."

How did the elder Davises keep this giant-sized brood in line?

"Both Mama and Papa handled the discipline. Sometimes I had whippings stacked up for days in advance. I'd stop Mama from cooking and ask, 'Can't I have at least two or three now and kind of get caught up?' Every time someone visited us, I got a whipping. I guess Mama wanted to show friends and relatives that she had us under control. It got so, when I saw company coming I'd break off a hickory limb, bring it to her, and say, 'Mama,

19

let's start.' You could hear my brothers and sisters scurrying under the house, banging their heads on the floors above. I believe it was good for me, taught me to behave and to treat company with respect."

And now it was time to start high school, which sounds simple enough except there wasn't one! Not only was there no school, but Jimmie says not a single person around even had a high school diploma.

The people of Beech Springs got together and passed a small tax in order to finally have a high school. Then, the people actually got hammers and saws and helped to build it. A man named Tyler from Jonesboro was chosen as contractor on the six-thousand-dollar job, which contained two stories, with an auditorium sharing half the upstairs space.

"We didn't have a piano for the auditorium right off," Davis recalls, "but someone was always bringing a fiddle or a guitar."

Of course, there was no library and almost no books. When a book was obtained, it was passed from family to family. But the school could boast of nine teachers, all graduates from Louisiana Industrial Institute of Ruston, which is now Louisiana Tech University.

A cottage was built for the teachers right across the road from school, and they were paid the handsome sum of eighty-five dollars a month.

One of Davis' teachers was Miss Lucille Long—now Lucille Hunt—a sister of Huey P. and Earl K. Long, who, like Davis, are now a part of Louisiana legend.

There is no way to measure the effect that these educated people had on Jimmie Davis. All of a sudden he was thrown into contact with people who knew something other than plowing someone else's land from dawn to dusk.

Some of the older school boys (and there were some students twenty-three years of age) courted the young lady teachers. Because going out on a school night was forbidden, the boys cleverly found a way to beat the rule. Possum hunting was not forbidden, and the boys began to take the teachers with them!

Davis says, "So many marriages were taking place as a result of all that possum-hunting courting, that we started taking preachers along to perform the ceremonies!"

Just how serious the problem became is witnessed by the fact that the local school board passed a law, which was put into each teacher's contract, prohibiting possum hunting any night but Saturday!

The Davis home, out in the country, was about two and one-half miles from the new school, and Jimmie recalls leaving for school many a morning at four-thirty in order to play some basketball before the bell rang. "Sometimes we played by moonlight."

The school played basketball and baseball. Davis remembers one basketball game they won by the score of 4–0, with his close friend Clyde Blaylock scoring all points.

> The game was so rough nobody wanted the ball!
>
> We didn't really know how to play and didn't have any equipment. We began with a hoop nailed to a sweet-gum tree. A teacher named Emmons suggested we get some real equipment from Sears in Chicago. Unfortunately the catalogue told us the ball cost $4.75, which we certainly didn't have. I couldn't even count that high. So we held a box supper and raised four dollars. Mr. Emmons put the last seventy-five cents up himself.
>
> Finally the big day came, and the ball arrived along with a small hand pump to blow it up. We

didn't understand that pump, were downright suspicious about it. We had a heavyset boy by the name of David Peel we trusted to blow up the ball with his mouth. He had that much wind. Well, Peel got the ball blown up, and there we were with a basketball with a snout sticking out. The snout was supposed to be stuck back inside the ball and the ball laced up.

We couldn't understand the instructions so we threw the laces away and left the snout sticking out. We threw the basketball by the snout from then on!

At that time we were allowed to play basketball with the girls. I was writing notes, of the roses-are-red, violets-are-blue variety, to one of the girls. Someone grabbed the snout, wound up like a base-ball pitcher, and threw the ball right at me. Without thinking, I hit it back. And wouldn't you know, it hit the girl I was writing to, right in the face, and knocked her flat on her back. She thought I'd done it on purpose. From that moment on, the boys stopped playing the girls.

The girls had their own basketball team and played in bloomers, big shapeless garments that hung like a sack. Davis believes that that era could well be called "the era of bloomers, outhouses, and churndashers."

They wore bloomers and high-top shoes because no one could afford tennis shoes. Some parents objected to the bloomers, though; they thought they were far too daring.

The first time I got a pair of tennis shoes, after wearing brogans all those years, I thought I could fly.

A teacher named Henry Harlan decided that the boys'

team needed uniforms. Harlan was a great teacher and a magnificent public speaker. Davis considers him his earliest inspiration and speaks reverently of him today.

We had five players and a substitute, and we went to the catalogue and ordered five suits. We didn't know the difference, and they sent us football uniforms complete with pads, shin guards, and helmets. We thought they were just fine and immediately put them on. I remember our smallest player who, because of his size, about five-feet-two, was the last to grab a uniform. He got a football outfit for a three-hundred-pound man. He wrapped the pants around himself twice, they came clear down to his ankles, and his jersey swallowed him up. When he put on his helmet, he looked exactly like a mule!

I remember the first time we saw a team in real basketball suits. It shocked us half to death. We thought they were naked! Early one freezing morning, our team got aboard a wagon and set out for the Parish (county) Rally in Jonesboro.

You can't imagine our effect on the crowd. We thought they were hysterically cheering for us, but they were really laughing their heads off at our outfits. I honestly believe we won the first game because the other team never got over its shock at our appearance. They'd try to shoot, but they'd fall apart laughing. We never noticed a thing. Then we won the second game. If it looked like we'd be beaten, the crowd would become threatening. Everyone wanted us in the finals because no one had ever seen a curiosity like that. The crowds got bigger and bigger, and sure enough we won the semifinals.

We got beat in the finals. We just couldn't make the adjustment to a basketball without a snout.

Don't forget, too, we had some pretty good-size boys, some of them twenty-three years of age, which didn't hurt either.

School work was something different. Davis just didn't like Latin. "I didn't know anybody I'd ever be able to speak to in Latin. A boy named Dawson Carson and I decided to do something about the problem, so early one morning we gathered up all the school's Latin books and hid them in a loft. Our Latin days were over, we thought. Miss Long suspected me, and a week later, when someone found the books, she picked one up and knocked me halfway across the room. I've respected Latin ever since."

Davis did like history and English, but most of all he liked the Friday Afternoon Society or talent shows put on in the auditorium. These shows consisted of recitations, spelling bees, debating, a reading of the school gossip (Johnny loves Suzie), and, most of all, musical numbers—solos, duets, and quartets. Assignments were given out a week in advance, and Jimmie was usually chosen for a duet or a quartet.

Songs included *Till We Meet Again, Little Rosewood Casket, Casey Jones, Wreck of the Old 97,* and *The Death of Floyd Collins.*

"Everybody would sing, and I was nothing special," he recalls. He does remember some enterprising classmates writing their own song, one based on a recent incident.

A boy named Chester Howard stepped on what looked like a rattlesnake, which bit him on the heel. Someone told him to cut open a live chicken and stick the wound in the chicken and tie it good and fast, which he did. He then took off running across the field, chicken and all, and later got well.

"My sister and the Stroud girls wrote a ditty:"

24

>As Chester did go
>Across the field
>A big old rattlesnake
>Bit him on the heel, etc.

Davis even remembers the tune.

His grades were average, and there was homework to be done by a fire from pine knots burning in the fireplace or by a kerosene lamp.

Nor could the unending farm chores be neglected. After school "you worked the field." Social life was not all that much, with Jump Josie (square dancing) at someone's home being a specialty.

Did they ever venture "far" from home? Jimmie Davis recalls only one such trip—a trip that might well have kept him close to Beech Springs forever.

"I was cutting stove wood with Papa. We sold it for one dollar a rick or three dollars a cord. Four of my friends came by and said they were going to the state fair in Shreveport, a distance of about eighty five miles. It sounded like China to me. The boys were Ernest Shows, Percy Bernard, Red Bridges, and David Peel. They would have to walk to Quitman, a distance of about six miles, and there catch a train.

>I looked at Papa for counsel, and he took a ten-dollar bill out of his jeans and said, "This is all I've got in the world and you can have it." Papa wasn't a hard man to love. Well, I'd never been on a train, and the first thing I saw on board was a man smoking a cigar. I wanted one, too. The only thing I had ever smoked was grape vine and corn silk. So I bought one for five cents, and it was the size of a Coke bottle. I commenced to puff on it the way I saw the man doing, and in a few minutes

I was so sick I wanted to die. In those days you could raise the window on trains, and it's a good thing because I leaned out the window and vomited through three towns!

We got to the fair, and you can just imagine a boy from Beech Springs. I was like a rabbit in New York City. The first thing I tried was throwing baseballs at wooden cats. I missed the cat completely and broke a kerosene lamp, scattering fire everywhere. The concessionaire told me to move on. But Ernest Shows was a good thrower. And before you knew it, he had knocked down enough cats to win a lavaliere, which he immediately put over his head.

The main attraction at the fair was a roller coaster, which back then was called a Scenic Railway. We got on, all of us in one seat. In the seat behind us were a couple of rather sizeable women, both of them about the size of small Buicks. For some reason, right as the ride began, Percy Bernard lit up a big cigar. He either spit the cigar out or bit it in two, because the next thing we knew, sparks flew back of us and set the two big women on fire.

A hot spark hit me too. I had a fuzzy, forty-nine-cent cotton shirt, and I commenced to go up in flames. I tore the shirt off and threw it away, and it landed on a lady behind the two heavy ones. She caught fire, too. By then there was general screaming, and people began to holler, look, and pray that the Scenic Railway would mercifully come to a stop.

It did, and the police were waiting for us as we stepped off. They took us to the calaboose, and when we got there we realized that Red Bridges had slipped away. For the moment we envied him.

They began to question us seriously. They were sure that Ernest Shows had stolen that lavaliere, and he begged them to accept his word that he'd won it moments before.

"Where you from?" they asked us. "Beech Springs," I said. "Where's that?" they asked. "Near Antioch," I told them. "Where's that?" they persisted. "Near Quitman," I swore. They said they'd never heard of any of those places. I explained what I thought would clear the matter up. "We're from between Antioch and Solemn Thought Church." They decided to keep us for the night.

At sunup they asked us if we were ready to go home. Were we ready? They gave us some directions. "Go directly to Texas Avenue, then to Crockett Street, and then. . . ." I had no idea what they were talking about. "Just point me," I begged, and they did. I had enough to get home on with a dime to spare. I wasn't sure they'd let me on the train without a shirt, so someone lent me a raincoat. When we got to the Shreveport depot, someone told us that Red Bridges had been killed at the west end of the Red River Bridge. Someone had cut his throat.

Red's casket got home on the train right after ours. I spent a sleepless night and the next day went to Red's funeral. When I finally got my feet into plowed ground, the back end of that mule looked better than anything I had ever seen in my life. I said to myself, not Shreveport or any other city will ever see me again. I'm staying out here where I belong.

In the tenth grade something happened to Jimmie that is not uncommon to the very young. He became certain that he knew enough. He could read and he could write;

he could even add and subtract. He and two other boys decided that the world needed them. Without saying anything to anyone, including their folks, they ran away from school and took a train to Winnfield. They had decided to be bank presidents!

Jimmie walked into the first bank he saw and asked to see the president. He told the man he'd like his job if the man was thinking of retiring. The president thanked him but told him he had no such immediate plans. Jimmie and his friends then hopped a freight to Alexandria, where they were certain fortune was waiting for them with open and money-filled arms.

They were absolutely convinced that the demand for their learning would be great and that they would have to sift carefully through the many offers they would receive.

Jimmie told Mr. Bolton who ran the bank that he'd like his job. After the man recovered from his shock, Davis recalls, he looked at the boy "like he thought I was crazy! They quickly shooed us out of the bank."

Jimmie and his friends lowered their employment sights a bit and wandered about town asking for employment at different stores. There, the story was the same.

> I told my friends that I didn't want to run out on them but that I had had enough, and if I could get back into school I'd take full advantage from now on. They said they were ready, too, and the three would-be bankers went home.
>
> When I got home, Papa was plowing in the field. I told him the whole story about my job failure. He asked me, "You want to go to school?" I told him I'd love to. He advised me to go tell the principal what had happened and to apologize for leaving. Papa said, "If he'll take you back, I'd

advise you to go to school; perhaps you've learned a lesson."

I learned more from my father, who had only a third grade education, than I ever learned from any college professor I ever had, and I say this with all respect to those professors because they were good to me. My father just knew how to say the right thing. He didn't push. He didn't order. He told you what he thought and what he believed, and almost all of the time he was right. I've long since realized that there are just some things you can't put in a book.

Now high school was drawing to a close, and it was time to consider what it was that a man might do with his life. There were not that many alternatives. A man might clerk in a store or be a blacksmith or even go on the road selling Watkins Products or stay a farmer or get a job in a sawmill.

There was still one other alternative—one that only Jimmie Davis considered.

A man might go to college.

Davis heard that the Bradley family, which lived three miles from his home, had something called a college catalogue.

"I was amazed and believed you could order a college just as you ordered something from Sears. I walked to the Bradleys' and borrowed the catalogue. I'd never seen a college, had never been on a college campus, but I read it and it told all about Louisiana College at Pineville. I decided that's where I would try to go."

Did Davis have any regrets about high school?

"It was good preparation, but it would have been so much better if we had had more books. I guess I was lucky. I didn't know how little I knew."

5. *The Big City—New Orleans*

New Orleans is often referred to as the city of seer-sucker suits, umbrellas, parades, and politicians the incubator where political rumors are born.

Between high school graduation and entering Louisiana College, Jimmie decided to have a look at something he'd always heard about: New Orleans. His trip is a legend of Jimmie Davis lore.

> I didn't have a suitcase, so I tied my clothes in a bed sheet and headed for the big town. After walking around with my mouth open for several hours, I stood on the corner of Canal and Royal streets just watching all the lights.
>
> At the same time I was looking for a restaurant sign. I was hoping to get me a bowl of chili or stew, but the lights were so fascinating I just kept looking. Why, up until this time I hadn't seen anything but the light of a kerosene lamp.

I looked down the street and saw Kolbs Restaurant. About the time I was ready to head for the restaurant, a pretty girl drove up in a big new car and said, "Would you like to go for a ride?" I said "No, I've got to go eat supper." I hated to turn her down because she was real friendly. As she drove off, right behind her came another girl, even prettier than the one before—all painted up, her hair hanging down to her waist. "Do you want to get in and go with me," she said. "No," I replied, "I've got to go eat." "Well that's all right," she said, "you can eat down at my place. We've got a big house and you can spend the night and I'll bring you back tomorrow morning." Everybody was so friendly, but I didn't go.

Finally I headed for Kolb's Restaurant. For some reason they seated me near the door.

I saw some people at the adjoining table drinking from a tall bottle, and I figured it was soda pop. I told the waiter I'd have one, too. I took one swig and couldn't swallow. I jumped from the table and raced out to the street and got rid of it. Beer! I'd never seen a bottle of beer in my life, much less drink one.

I gathered up my courage and went on back in. The waiter handed me a menu, and I didn't know what to do with it, so I used it as a fan. I didn't know what to ask for, but I spotted the people at the next table eating something and I said, "Give me some of that." To this day I don't know what it was, but I ate it.

I noticed that as people got up from their tables, they left money which I saw the waiter pick up. I put a nickel on the table. The waiter saw it and went into what looked like shock. Now it's a long way from the front of Kolb's to the back, but he hauled off and bounced that nickel off the back wall. He didn't know how much that nickel meant to me.

I walked out front and by then it had gotten dark and I saw a light in the sky. I spotted a policeman and asked him, "What's that?" He explained that it was a searchlight advertising a dance-excursion steamboat. I'd never heard of anything like that—a boat that you could dance on! I asked the officer, "Can anybody go?" He said, "If you've got seventy-five cents." I said, "I got it."

So I followed the light and got aboard this huge boat. Loud music was playing and everybody was dancing, swaying, and dipping but me and three other wallflowers who sat together on a bench. I decided to get me one of them. I picked out a long tall, pretty brunette. It was the first time I'd ever attempted to dance in my life.

She asked me if I'd ever danced before, and I replied no. She said she didn't think so. I wrapped my right arm around her, and that was the first woman I'd ever held in my arms except my mama. Let me tell you, the first time you do something like that, it's a funny feeling.

That was the slipperiest dance floor I've seen in all my life. I was desperately trying to imitate what I saw others doing, and we both started sliding on that slippery floor. We were sliding right between dancing couples, and I was trying not to kill anyone, and in all this carrying on I swung her so high she could see over the entire crowd.

By this time her stomach was on my head, and she was clearing the way head first. I knew we had to turn a corner up ahead because the distance was only about two hundred feet. We had to try!

We knocked down two couples, and she landed

flat on her back with my right knee in the middle of her stomach with all my hundred and seventy-five pounds behind it. Her eyes crossed and her tongue stuck out and her dress was up around her neck, and I said, "My Lord, I've killed her."

The other girls on the bench, her sisters, were following us because they knew somebody was going to get hurt. Along with a brother or a cousin, they picked her up and got her dress straightened out and stretched her out on a bench. They put cold towels to her head, and finally she came to. She looked at me and screamed. I didn't say a word. I didn't know what to do because that cruise had another two hours to go. That's the longest two hours I ever spent.

The whole time she kept looking back over her shoulder at me and wondering what she'd gotten herself into. I sat there until the boat got within ten feet of the bank, and I jumped off into the water knee deep. I kept right on going, got my clothes together and headed for home.

When I got there, Papa said, "Back a little early, aren't you?" I said, "I'm afraid I killed a woman." He asked, "Did you shoot her?" I said, "No." Then he asked, "Did you cut her?" I said, "No, I did it dancing." Papa replied, "That must have been some dance."

I said, "Yes it was, and from now on I'm sticking to square dancing. I don't want my arms around any other woman as long as I live!"

6. *College*

The problem was simple if the solution was not. How to go to college?

"I didn't have any money and I didn't know anybody who did. I decided to get a job at the college."

With five dollars in his pocket and a "please-don't-rain" suitcase borrowed from an older sister, Jimmie hopped a freight train for Alexandria late one afternoon, having been told that the train usually stopped at the Louisiana College Junction a couple of miles from Alexandria.

> It was pitch black, and I suddenly realized that the train wasn't slowing down. I grabbed my suitcase and jumped like a flying squirrel. When I hit the ground, my suitcase burst open, sending Vaseline hair tonic, shoe polish, antiseptic, Cloverine Salve, and chill tonic scattering for seventy-five yards up and down the embankment. I scram-

bled about in the dark trying to get my possessions together and ended up with the suitcase about half full of rocks.

I saw a light up ahead and had the sense to go to it. It was a house, and I knocked on the door and asked instructions to the college. The man pointed up ahead to a brick building, where I immediately went. A lady came to the door, and I explained that I wanted a room. She said, "Son, this is a girls' dormitory." I said, "That'll be all right. I'm not looking to get married, just for a place to lie down." I'm lucky she didn't call the police. Instead she directed me to the boys' dormitory.

I was three days early, and there were only three other boys in the whole building. I got a room. Down the hall was a strange object the likes of which I had never seen. A shower! After a couple of hours I mastered the art of regulating the water, and I stood on a bench to get cleaned off. Don't you know I slipped and hit my head on the concrete floor? I literally saw sparks flying. It was several days before I worked up the courage to go near that thing again.

The next day Jimmie went to the college employment office and found odd jobs washing dishes in the school kitchen and working in people's yards.

College was beyond a doubt the truly formative period of Jimmie Davis' life. It was there that he found himself, a person who could mix well and get along with other people; he found that he had the ability to entertain others, and most important of all, he found formal religion that was to be the cornerstone of his life.

The boy from outside Beech Springs found college to be a strange experience. "I didn't know there were that many people in the world. I must say, though, that people were extremely kind and understanding, and if they noticed my threadbare clothes, they never let me know it."

Needless to say, the transition from a rural high school to college was extremely difficult. "I had to start from scratch. Because we didn't have a library back home, I simply had no idea of how to use one or for that matter what one even was. I stayed after every class getting extra help, and I had to study through just about every night. I wasn't trying to do well; I just wanted to get caught up. I very seldom went home. I knew that if I had any future at all, it wasn't in Beech Springs. My grades that first semester were just average, and maybe that's bragging a bit.

"If it wasn't for some awfully understanding teachers, of course, there was no way that I could have made it. Fortunately they could tell that I was sincere, I really wanted to learn. I just started so far back that if they had discouraged me, there's no way that I could have made it. They were never anything but kind."

Jimmie tried out for the basketball team and made it, but a bad back prevented him from continuing. Maybe that was a blessing, because he had little spare time and wanted to use it productively. He joined the glee club. Professor Dunwoody soon assigned him to the college quartet.

Jimmie sang lead. Other quartet members were Paul Culpepper, first tenor; Charley Roberts, baritone; and Chet Steadman, bass. Professor Dunwoody gave the boys a program of classical songs to learn, but Jimmie says, "I just couldn't feel our audiences responding to them. We didn't understand them, and neither did most of our listeners. I suggested to the professor that the quartet do just a few lighter numbers and spirituals. He agreed, and we set out to learn *I Shall Not Be Moved, Ain't Going to Study War No More,* and some favorites like *Dear Old Girl* and *Down by the Old Mill Stream.* It was obvious that that's exactly the kind of music the audiences wanted to hear!"

At about that time Jimmie Davis received one of the significant gifts of his life. His oldest sister's husband, Carl Watson, gave him a much-used guitar, and Jimmie taught himself to play it. Now the boy from Beech Springs could not only sing but could accompany himself as well.

The quartet performed for neighboring churches and schools, and kindly families let them spend the night in their homes. Davis recalls "one swanky house we stayed in that had a ceiling fan."

"It was wintertime, and for some reason the thing was on. We pressed one button, but that only made it go faster. Finally we gave up; there was no way we were going to master anything that complicated. We froze all night under that big fan."

Jimmie was now desperate for money with which to stay in school. He hit upon an idea to try and make some that was to change his life forever, although he certainly didn't know it at the time.

With guitar in hand, he began to sing on street corners in Alexandria. Kindly strangers gave him a few coins. "Sometimes an officer broke up the crowd and told me to go home. But I was desperate. If I didn't make some change, I knew I wouldn't eat, so I just moved on to another corner and started up again. I don't know if people were paying me to sing or shut up! Once in a while I'd make six or seven dollars a day! I never considered being an entertainer. I was just trying to stay together."

Despite these financial hard times there is much evidence that the Davis brand of humor was already in full bloom. Consider this Davis memory:

> In college I met a cute girl who I really wanted to date and I had the impression that the feeling was mutual. Finally I worked up the courage and said to her, "I'd love to have a date with you tonight but I just haven't got the money." She replied, "I do and I've got my daddy's car. You can drive." I said, "No, I'll kill both of us. You drive."
>
> First we went to a picture show and then to the Owl Drug Store in Pineville. J.C. Hines, (now deceased), a friend of mine who roomed across the hall in the dorm, walked in with his date and sat with us. J.C. said, "The treats on me!" Well everybody but me ordered soda drinks that I'd never heard of. They just didn't make 'em at Beech Springs. I was looking at the drug store shelves and just for fun and to embarrass J.C. a little I said, "Bring me a bottle of that Pluto Water" (a well known laxative).
>
> J.C. took me seriously and said to the waitress, "Oh no young lady, don't do that; bring him a milkshake." I said I'd settle for that.
>
> Until his last day on this earth J.C. never did know I knew the difference. He never would double date with me again, saying, "Jimmie, you'll embarrass us all to death."
>
> For a long time friends called me Pluto and once in class a professor even addressed me that way. I said, "You mean Plato." "No," the professor replied, "I said Pluto!"

Jimmie recalls another college story with himself, as usual, the butt of the joke.

> I had been dating a girl who lived in Arcadia, Louisiana, which called for a rather lengthy train

ride. One Saturday I left Alexandria on the train
and had to change trains at Winnfield which called
for a mile walk to another depot. I got on board
and sat next to a young man who introduced himself as Harold Weston and said that he was teaching
in central Louisiana. We chatted pleasantly until
we arrived at Ruston where we both got off the
train to catch still another train for Arcadia.

Once again we found ourselves sitting together
and once again we resumed our conversation. The
train finally arrived at Arcadia and we both got off.
Weston mentioned that he had a date with a local
girl and I said, "So have I!" We both started
walking towards a house on a hill and I said,
"That's where my date lives." Weston said that
was where his date lived too. I asked him her name
and when he told me I said, "Friend, we've got a
date with the same girl!" He said, "Let's not worry
about it." I said, "No, I won't worry, if she's
making dates with two fellows at the same time,
you take her and I'll take her roommate." He
said, "No, we'll flip a coin. Heads, I get the date,
and tails I get the roommate."

The coin spun in the air, landed . . . and there
I was, stuck with a two-timing girl! When I was
finally alone with her, I said, "Will you please tell
me what's going on here?" Then I said, "No, don't
do it, there's not going to be a wedding anyway so
it's best that I should never know. The four of us
will just go ahead and have a ball."

And we did.

Major events in people's lives seldom enter with a
flourish. One day Jimmie was walking across campus and
he met another man, "handsome, well dressed, and middle aged."

We introduced ourselves. He was Dr. Robert G. Lee, pastor of Bellevue Baptist Church in Memphis and three times president of the Southern Baptist Convention. Dr. Lee was holding a revival in Pineville.

I had always gone to church but had never really thought about becoming a Christian. At first we talked about football and baseball. Dr. Lee said, "Jimmie, can I ask you something? If the Lord would call you today, would you be ready to go?" I said, "Dr. Lee, I hope He doesn't call me today because I don't think I could make it." "Well," he replied, "the Lord's been good to you, and it's something you ought to think about." He closed by saying, "I hope you'll come to church tonight."

I didn't tell him yes or no, but when I got back to my room, the more I thought about it the more I realized I wasn't ready to go. I realized that everything I had, everything I had ever had, and everything I would ever hope to have on this earth had come and would come through the grace of God. I thought, it's only through the grace of God that I wasn't killed in a car wreck last night or didn't die of a heart attack instead of somebody else.

So that night I went to church. Dr. Lee gave one of his most famous and beloved sermons, *Pay Day, Some Day*. There's no doubt of it, the man had the finest command of the English language that I have ever heard. Before he had finished, I was ready to go down the aisle. And when he gave the invitation, I was the first one down and made public my profession of faith and united with that church.

On the subject of religion, Davis' thinking has not changed from that long ago night in Pineville, Louisiana.

41

"Every man needs God as a partner because you can't make it by yourself. I knew that it was my duty to try and contribute something to life, not just take from it, and I determined to try to be a better citizen. I hadn't been all that bad, but I had done nothing for the Man who did so much for me. I believe that was the most important thing I learned at Louisiana College or for that matter in all my life. It was something that lasted and the only thing I can take with me when I leave this earth."

In his third year at Louisiana College, a sad truth became obvious to Jimmie Davis. He simply did not have the money to continue. And worse, he couldn't borrow any.

He tried banks for a loan, but when they asked for collateral, the young man from Beech Springs had to admit he just didn't have any. The loan was denied. Jimmie looks at it this way. "Everybody ought to be hungry and try to borrow money at least once in their life. To be broke and turned down, well, it's something!"

Jimmie Davis dropped out of Louisiana College and went back to something he had hoped with all his heart he'd never have to do again—work someone else's land.

Back home a farmer named Alex Rasbury had a small hill farm that he told Jimmie he could work on halves. The farm consisted of meager acreage and a sorghum-fed mule named Kate.

The college boy found himself back of a mule again, plowing and picking cotton from sunup to sunset. He made three bales of cotton, which was then selling for ten cents a pound. A bale weighed five hundred pounds, and Rasbury and Jimmie each made seventy-five dollars. Jimmie supplemented this by slipping back into Alexandria whenever he could and singing on those street corners. He stayed out of college one year.

Did he ever consider not returning? "Never. I was discouraged, of course. It's kind of hard starting over, but I knew what I wanted. I figured that maybe I could become a teacher and even save up enough money to buy my own small farm. That was absolutely the only career that occurred to me at that time.

"People were extremely kind, though. One professor, Willie Strother, a history teacher, lent me a hundred and twenty dollars. By the time I got out of college, I must have owed everybody I had ever met.

"I recall a barber in Jonesboro, A. C. Holly, who later became the Mayor. He told me, 'Son, if you ever need a little money, write a check on me.' I must have written fifty checks on A. C. Holly. When I became Governor, he was one of the first men I gave a job to."

So, with borrowed money, with money from farming, and with money from the street corners of Alexandria, Jimmie Davis graduated from Louisiana College. No member of the Davis family attended graduation exercises. They simply didn't have the time or the clothes to wear.

7. *A Break . . . At Last!*

After college Jimmie returned to Beech Springs. He recalls his father meeting him at the depot and bringing him home in the old family wagon. His parents were very proud of the new graduate. They knew nothing whatever of what he had been through to get that degree.

"They knew I had something no one else around had, but they didn't know how I'd gotten it. I hadn't shared my problems with them. Perhaps I hadn't even been aware that I had had problems. Sweating it out was our way of life."

What was Jimmie's own reaction to having an education? "At long last I realized how much I didn't know!"

There was one logical job open for him, and he became his rural high school's first graduate to return as a teacher. Many of the kids were not much younger than their teacher. "I could relate to them in every way, and I believe that made me more able to assist them. I was even able to encourage several of them to go on to college, which made me especially proud."

Davis taught all subjects and coached basketball. By now the team had real uniforms, and the snout was no longer protruding from the basketball. "I guess you could say we had made some progress." Jimmie was paid about ninety-five dollars a month and lived with his folks and the other children in the family cabin.

After school he worked the fields the same as always. There were plenty of mouths to feed, and everyone— even a "brand-new educator"—had to get back of the mule.

Jimmie Davis wasn't through with getting his own education yet. Almost immediately he began to save what he could in order to pursue a master's degree from Louisiana State University at Baton Rouge. He didn't discuss these aspirations with anyone because "it would have taken so long to explain what a Master's was, and besides, I'm not sure I exactly knew."

Though not a member, Davis was allowed to live in a loft in the Alpha Gamma Rho agricultural fraternity house. He shared the loft with Howard Clayton from Jonesboro. There was no heater and little light. Jimmie Davis did one other thing as he sought this advanced degree. He hit the street corners of Baton Rouge with his guitar to make a few dollars. In one year he was awarded his master's degree in education.

It's interesting to note that at that period, politics held no interest for him whatever, and music was only a way to make eating money.

Jimmie returned to Shreveport, where he taught at Dodd College, a girls' school.

"Well, now, that was a new experience. I wasn't much

older than my students, and let me tell you, you can learn more teaching than you can going to school! When you teach a class of freshman girls, you better be ready. They came up with questions that a physician couldn't answer, much less someone fresh out of Beech Springs!"

While Davis taught at Dodd College, he lived in a fraternity house in Shreveport. Across the street lived Public Service Commissioner Huey Pierce Long. On several occasions the young professor accompanied the budding politician on walks. Davis recalls one such walk in particular.

"Huey said to me that perhaps one day I might consider participating in politics. I thanked him for what I guess was a compliment, but I said I thought I'd stick to teaching."

Fate had other plans, and Jimmie Davis was to serve exactly as Huey Long had, as public service commissioner and then governor.

Right about that time Jimmie Davis began doing something on a casual, hobby-like basis which was to change his life forever. In his spare time he began to write songs.

What Jimmie's young lady students didn't know was that their teacher was the same "Jimmie" who sang every Friday night on KWKH Radio.

W. K. Henderson, owner of KWKH, had heard Jimmie sing and invited him to do a weekly program. Jimmie's accompanist was James Enloe of Mansfield. Jimmie sang both pop and country songs, including numbers like *My Blue Heaven,* all the Jimmy Rogers yodeling tunes, and *When It's Prayer Meeting Time in the Hollow.*

When the station began to be flooded with mail about the young singer known only as "Jimmie," KWKH began paying him about five dollars for a Friday night show that could last anywhere from two to three hours.

Here, fate stepped in. A talent scout for a number of recording companies heard Davis sing and tipped off Decca Records (now MCA Decca) that "maybe this kid has something." Decca wrote Jimmie a letter asking him to come to Memphis for a tryout. The catch was that Jimmie Davis didn't get the letter for six months as it lay on someone's desk.

When he finally did get it, he immediately wrote Decca, "I just got your letter and if you still want me to come, I'm ready." David Kapp, Decca vice president, responded that he was going to Chicago to record someone and if Jimmie wanted to come up he'd give him an audition.

Jimmie gathered up some of his own songs and went to Chicago. "I had one number in particular I wanted to do, but they didn't think too much of it. Finally, they let me do it."

That number was *Nobody's Darling but Mine,* and not only did it earn Jimmie a two-year option with Decca, but the song became a hit. Jimmie remembers his accompanying musicians on that first big record. Warren Pottinger of Amarillo, Texas, played the dobro (nonelectric steel guitar), and Tex Swain of Ardmore, Oklahoma, was on the standard guitar.

Not only was Jimmie's own recording of his tune a hit, but Gene Autry, who then had a nationwide radio show every Sunday, had a hit with it, too, as did Bing Crosby, Guy Lombardo, Wayne King, the Andrew Sisters, and a dozen more famous artists.

With the money from this tune, Jimmie purchased a 100-acre farm outside Shreveport. The sharecropper wasn't a sharecropper any more.

Six months later Jimmie recorded his second hit, *Where the Old Red River Flows.*

At about that time Jimmie's life veered off onto another course that was to be as important to him as his uniquely blossoming music career.

Jimmie had become friends with Judge David B. Samuel of Shreveport, who offered the young teacher and singer a job as clerk of the criminal court. Jimmie accepted, and not yet wise in the ways of politics, particularly Louisiana politics, didn't know that his job would include being the "hatchet man" in the judge's next election.

The "hatchet man" in any campaign not only has to answer charges, of which there are always hundreds, but make a few hundred against the opposition as well.

"I remember the first time Judge Samuel asked me to speak for him. 'What'll I tell 'em?' I asked him. 'Tell them I'm a good man,' the judge suggested," and Jimmie did just that in the very first political speech he ever made, in a garage in the Queensboro subdivision.

The campaign was an interesting one. The judge's opponents charged him with "fining someone and then, if they were first offenders, suspending part or all of the fine." In other words, they said "he was too easy on the guilty."

Jimmie recalls one of his own "hatchet" speeches about the opposing candidate. "I pointed out that the opposition, a lawyer, had represented the biggest 'blind tiger' beer bootlegger ever to come before the court and proudly displayed his plea for a suspended sentence for his client who'd been in the same trouble numerous times before!

"Did I like to do that kind of speaking? In no way.

But I was with the judge, sink or swim. It's the only way I ever played politics."

It should be noted that that campaign was Jimmie Davis' single endeavor as a "hatchet man." It simply was not his style, and from then on his role in campaigns personified the exact opposite approach: never demeaning any opponent or, for that matter, even mentioning them.

Judge Samuel beat the field, and Jimmie Davis continued to perform his court duties, in addition to singing on KWKH and making one-night appearances in neighboring towns.

By then Jimmie traveled with his own band, which included Charles Mitchell on the steel guitar; Mitchell's wife on the ukelele; Herschell Woodall on bass; Tex Swain on guitar; and Bill Harper on the fiddle. Jimmie and the band were much in demand, and there was no city or community in the northern part of the state where they did not perform.

While they were performing, the young entertainer was meeting a lot of people, shaking a lot of hands, and establishing a reputation as a good man. The fruits of these labors were eventually to include being elected Governor of Louisiana, but that was to come later.

Davis also did a great deal of public speaking. His subject was either music or what was going on in the criminal court in Shreveport.

Once when Jimmie got a two-week vacation, he and the band loaded up the rack on the back of an old car with their luggage. Then the five band members got inside with their instruments for the long ride to California, where Jimmie had a recording date.

When they got to Pineville, Louisiana, the rack broke, scattering their luggage "from Louisiana College to the

Alexandria bridge." The inside of the car now included five people, their instruments, and their luggage.

"When we were going through the desert, I didn't think we'd make it," Jimmie recalls.

Jimmie remembers one appearance in Lake Charles, Louisiana, where he sat by the radio with a theater owner, an Englishman, and heard the Duke of Windsor abdicate his throne "for the woman I love." "The Englishman wept throughout the speech. I don't believe any of us really understood exactly what was going on. I gather Wally and the Duke understood just fine. Their marriage certainly indicates that."

Now Jimmie and the band were adding benefit performances to their one night stands. If a neighboring town, church, or school had a worthy project, they'd help out. Jimmie Davis was becoming a definite factor in the world he inhabited.

8. *A Bride and a New Job*

A friend of Jimmie's, Lyman McBride, was dating a girl named Mary White, a teacher. McBride invited Jimmie to join him and his date for a game of bridge, explaining that they'd get him a blind date.

She was Alvern Adams, a graduate of Centenary College and a young teacher. Alvern was the daughter of Mrs. W. M. Adams and the late Dr. Adams.

I enjoyed that first date and said we'd have to do it again. And we began to date. We'd go to a picture show, and on Sunday we'd go to church. I'm afraid Alvern wasn't all that taken with my country brand of music. The truth of the matter is, she was a wee bit sophisticated in her music.

We decided to get married, and the ceremony took place in Alvern's home with the immediate family and two clergymen, Dr. George Sexton, president of Centenary College, and Dr. M. E.

Dodd, pastor of the First Baptist Church, to which I belonged.

It was in April and still pretty cool, and I had only one suit, a thin one. So I slipped my pajamas on under my suit. I guess I'm the only man ever to get married in his pajamas. It wasn't much of a suit, and I know for sure it wouldn't have stood another wedding!

We decided to go to Tyler, Texas, on our honeymoon. When we got started on the car trip, I asked my new bride, "Got any money?" She said she had thirty dollars, and I told her that was twenty-six dollars more than I had! About then my wife pointed below the cuffs of my pants to where my pajamas were sticking out. "What's that?" she asked. I explained about my pajamas and the cold weather, and I told her that getting married was the very first experience I'd had like that.

We got to Tyler and looked at the rose gardens and ate some stew at the hotel. We returned to Shreveport the next afternoon because the money had run out!

We moved in with Mrs. Adams. We paid her fifty dollars a month for room, board, and laundry. Mrs. Adams was like a mother to me, treated me like her own son. In fact, living there was so good, that's where we stayed until I was elected Governor.

I walked to and from work every day unless somebody gave me a ride. It took me seven years to pay off all my debts and to be able to buy a car.

My problem was I needed a better job, and one came open—police commissioner of Shreveport. The difficulty was I'd have to run for it. Lal Blanchard, the former district attorney, was the incumbent; he and Roscoe Cranor, a state senator, were my opponents. Cranor was supported by the

then Louisiana Governor Dick Leche and the old
Huey P. Long faction.

Out of this campaign was born the Jimmie Davis style
of politicking, unique to the man and to the times he
ran in.

Jimmie decided to use his band to draw a crowd.
While this proved a blessing, it also proved to be a trap
from which he was never to escape. Jimmie Davis simply
could not appear without a band. People *liked* his speaking. They *loved* his singing. There was never again to be
simply a speech; there had to be guitar and fiddle present
or the crowd felt let down, in some way cheated of something they loved.

> We drew huge crowds as we'd set up, sing some,
> and speak some. After a while other candidates
> asked us if they could appear with us. We said okay
> and that we'd give them three minutes, but we used
> a "coattail snatcher," someone whose job was
> pulling on the speaker's coattails and telling him,
> "You've got a minute," "Now thirty seconds," and
> so on. Sometimes the "coattail snatcher" would
> pull the candidate off the stage and he'd still be
> talking. We had to do it that way. Some would
> have spoken for hours!
>
> The campaign was a tough one, with all of the
> power against me with the exception of one city
> councilman, Bob Allen.
>
> We heard the election returns at Max Goldberg's
> World Champion Shoe Shop in downtown Shreve-
> port. When it became obvious that we'd won, we
> went on home to the Adamses. No big celebration,
> no banquets. As I recall, we ate some turnip greens
> and cornbread.

Jimmie Davis had been elected to his first public office.
A legend was being born.

9. *Hollywood and More Politics*

At about the same time Jimmie was in California for a recording session, when Decca executive Jack Kapp asked him if he wanted to join him for lunch in the Universal Pictures Commissary. Kapp didn't mention that his other guest would be Cliff Work, president of Universal, and actress Deanna Durbin.

Jimmie recalls meeting a young actress named Rita Hayworth in the commissary. "She was a beautiful girl, very vivacious, and I've got to admit I really hadn't seen too many like her where I grew up."

Work asked the country singer if he'd like to be in a movie. Jimmie, who still had some vacation time, said he'd try it and was told to report on Monday.

The picture was *Strictly in the Groove* and starred Ozzie and Harriet Nelson, whom Davis remembers as "a fine couple," and the Denning Sisters.

Jimmie realized that he needed an agent to handle his

growing musical career, so he called Mitch Hamilburg, who was Gene Autry's agent. "I introduced myself on the phone, and he suggested that he'd never heard of me. I was about to get a brush-off when I told him I had already been in a picture and I only wanted someone to go and collect my money. He saw the light and said, 'I'll be over in thirty seconds.' "

The Davis–Hamilburg combination was to last for years and was to do well by both men.

The movie people asked Jimmie if he could ride a horse, and he told them he was a country boy and had "practically been raised on one."

He was offered a part in a Western. His role would consist of him singing a few songs and taking part in the chase scene as the posse went after the bad guys. The movie starred Charles Starrett, then a reigning Western hero.

Jimmie was sent to the costume shop to get outfitted in cowboy regalia. "They gave me one of those Buck Jones-old hats. It must have been a size nine and was jet black. It hung almost around my neck, and I couldn't see a thing. Then they strapped on a pair of six-shooters and I was all set. I thought.

> Each of us was assigned a horse for the posse scene, and since I was a newcomer, the boys decided to play a little trick on me. I got a big black horse that specialized in bucking. Of course, I didn't know it.
>
> The scene opened with all of us good guys in the cafe. Someone rushed in and shouted, "They've just robbed the bank!" We shouted, "Let's get 'em!" All fifteen of us ran out the small cafe door at the same time and with much shouting jumped on our horses. It was then that I made my error.

I stuck the spurs into my horse, and he commenced bucking and generally going crazy.

First, both my six-shooters flew off, each in an opposite direction. With that hat over my face, I couldn't see a thing. The horse bucked and reared, and I hung on for dear life. Finally they got me off, and the man who was in charge of the horses was some angry because he realized I could have been killed. I walked around for the rest of the day as if holding "on to the saddle." I thought I was still on that horse.

Of course, they had to shoot the scene over, and this time I tied the six-shooters around my legs and even got a hat that fit. I also got a horse I could ride.

Jimmie got parts in a half dozen other Westerns, always playing the "good buddy" to some cowboy star. They included Charles Starrett, Jimmy Wakely, and Tex Ritter.

He was offered the opportunity to remain in Hollywood and stay in pictures, but he refused. "I always knew I belonged in Louisiana."

What he didn't know was that the next movie he made, a few years later, would be the story of one Jimmie Davis!

By now Jimmie had been police commissioner for four years and had spent a lot of that time studying government and wondering where he might fit in.

"I wanted to be someplace non-controversial. I simply liked people too much to get involved in anything too hectic. At least that's what I thought at that time."

Jimmie decided to run for the Louisiana Public Service Commission, the state agency that regulates utilities, railroads, all public carriers, and truck lines.

The Public Service Commission was divided into geographic districts, and the district that Jimmie would run for had once been represented by one Huey P. Long, who went from there to the Governor's Mansion. Davis says he never considered this.

The race would be a tough one, with the incumbent, John S. Patton, heavily backed by the always-powerful Long faction.

It was in this race that Jimmie discovered a campaign manager who, as long as she lived, played a dominant role in Jimmie Davis' never (until she passed away) losing a race.

Alvern Davis "took over" the campaign, wrote the advertising, arranged the speaking itinerary, and paid the bills.

Her main attribute as a politician, in addition to a brilliant mind, was a memory that Louisiana politicians still refer to as "phenomenal." It's said that Alvern Davis never forgot a name.

Jimmie won the race by more than thirty thousand votes over all candidates and now had increased his constituency to some twenty-six parishes (counties), a little less than half of the state.

As Jimmie's career blossomed, so did his musical life. During this period Jimmie and his band leader Charlie Mitchell wrote a tune called *You Are My Sunshine,* which remains today one of the three most popular songs ever written.

The song has been recorded more than three hundred and fifty times by artists in every musical style from pop (Bing Crosby and Guy Lombardo) to soul (Ray Charles and Aretha Franklin). Jimmie has heard it performed accompanied by primitive tom-toms and by a hundred-piece orchestra in Carnegie Hall.

10. *Governor*

Louisiana Governor Sam Houston Jones, a reform candidate who had defeated the Long machine, was nearing the end of his term and had a problem. At that time Louisiana's constitution did not allow a governor to succeed himself in office, and Jones was looking for a successor who would protect the reforms he felt he had initiated.

For most of his term, Jones had been promoting A. P. "Pat" Tugwell, state treasurer, to succeed him. But adverse publicity, in the hands of the opposition, removed Tugwell from consideration.

Now Jones and his advisors turned their eyes to Shreveport, where Jimmie Davis had just been elected to the Public Service Commission in the first primary. Davis had few if any political scars and was widely known through his music on almost every jukebox in the state.

Jones sent two high-ranking officials to north Louisiana

to discuss the matter with Davis. They were Prescott Foster, son of former Governor and U.S. Senator Murphy Foster, and D. Y. Smith, director of the Louisiana Department of Highways and a founding director of Delta Airlines. Davis refused to see them.

He explains, "I was enjoying my work on the commission and making records. I simply didn't want all those worries."

Davis went to Baton Rouge for a commission meeting, where Lee Laycock, clerk of the Louisiana House of Representatives and a Jones assistant, asked if he could see him. That was Jimmie Davis' first visit to the governor's office.

> Laycock said that the governor, who was visiting David Lide's farm on Lake Bruin near Newellton, wanted to see me, and if I'd go, he, Laycock, would drive me up there and then on to my home in Shreveport. I said okay.
>
> We got to Lake Bruin, and Governor Jones was dangling his feet in the water. We shook hands, and he said some of his friends would like to see me run for governor and he was for it, too. I said, "Governor, for the first time in my life I don't owe anybody, I'm out of debt, and I like it that way. Also, two things bother me about the governor's job. First, the oil business scares me. The potential for scandal is so great that I'd want to stay completely clear of it. Secondly, I don't want to take any heat about gambling. It's prevalent throughout the state, and you and I know that in some parts of the state it's just a way of life. Well, I'm for home rule, not interfering with local law officials unless asked to or unless there's a complete breakdown of law enforcement."

Jones explained that a governor no longer had to be

interjected into the state's oil business. The Mineral Board (of which the governor is an ex-officio member) takes care of that.

"Jones was right about that. During the eight years that I served as governor, I went to only one Mineral Board meeting, and that was only because they needed me to make up a quorum."

On the issue of gambling, which Jones had campaigned against, he explained that the people picked up in the state police raids had either been given ridiculously light sentences or set completely free after only the most minimal of trials. Jones said, "I guess the best thing on that subject is just to let them handle their own business."

Davis promised the Governor that he'd think it over, and he returned to Shreveport and a waiting Alvern about midnight. The couple had a talk that Davis will never forget.

Davis said, "I think I'm going to get in the governor's race and I think I can win. They're going to say some awful things about me, Alvern. The bad part is they're going to have you believing it before it's over. They may have me believing it!" Alvern replied, "It's just you and me. I don't care whether you politick, preach, or plow. If you want to run, I'm with you."

The next day Jimmie went to discuss the matter with his father. Jones Davis had these words. "If you want to go, go, but the only thing worse than losing will be winning! You'll be in some fast company and just remember, when you're dancing with a bear, keep your eyes on your partner!"

Davis, always slow to make up his mind, returned to Baton Rouge still undecided. Governor Jones called a meeting at the Governor's Mansion attended by all of his department heads and close friends and Jimmie Davis.

At the meeting Jones said that because Jimmie wasn't a political speaker, he and other high administration officials would be happy to go out and speak for him.

At that point Jimmie Davis declared an independence that no one in the room knew he possessed.

He said, "Governor, I'm deeply appreciative of your offer, and I respect you as a gentleman, but if you or any other big wheel speak for me, I'll get out of the campaign. I'll do my own speaking in my own way. I don't believe the people will go for the show of a lot of power. People want to make up their own minds."

Davis told the group that he estimated it would take about seventy-five thousand dollars to get the campaign underway. They replied, "Today's Friday; you announce tomorrow, and we'll have the money to you on Monday."

"To this day I'm still waiting for that money," Jimmie Davis says. He still had a lot to learn about politics and political promises!

Davis' opposition was awesome. The Long faction decided that Earl K. Long would not be their best candidate for governor. Instead, they let him run for lieutenant governor. To lead their ticket they chose a former congressman, Lewis Morgan. Congressman Jimmy Morrison of Hammond, surely the toughest campaigner of his time, also entered the race, as did Vincent Mosely of Opelousas and a really unique figure in all Louisiana political history, Dudley J. LeBlanc of Abbeville.

This was the same LeBlanc who was later to amass a fortune as the inventor of the cure-all elixir, Hadacol. At the time of this race, LeBlanc's medical sights were not set so high, and he was offering the public only two cures: Dixie Dew Cough Syrup and Happy Day Headache Powders.

A strong backer of the Morgan-Long ticket was long-time New Orleans Mayor Robert Maestri and all but two elected officials in New Orleans, where one-third of the state's vote lay.

As the campaign was about to get underway, Davis was leaving the Public Service Commission office, when a young commission employee, Chris Faser, suitcase in hand, got into Davis' car.

"Where are you going?" Davis asked him. "With you," Faser replied. "Okay," Davis said, and one of the closest personal and political relationships was born. Faser was to be like Davis' son. He proved to be a brilliant political operative, perhaps the best of his time.

The campaign was to be a combination of the humorous and the brutal; it was also to see the unique Davis style of campaigning come into full bloom. It was not a style that anyone would ever be able to copy, because it was built around Jimmie Davis' lovely baritone voice.

Jimmie first gathered a band. He went to Port Arthur, Texas, where he enticed piano player Moon Mulligan, a long-time friend of Jimmie's, to leave his saloon and join up. From south Louisiana he recruited Doc Guidry, "King of the Cajun Fiddlers," and on the guitar were Joe Shelton and others.

To Jimmie, music meant a few moments of relaxation—a way to forget politics for the time being. Sometimes when Jimmie would get real tired on the campaign trail, he'd come to some town where a large crowd had gathered for the speaking. Jimmie would walk to the microphone and say: "My friends, no speaking today—it'll all be singing. But don't you worry and have no fear, for we are gonna fix all of you up anyway. So gather 'round and let's get the show on the road." And the crowd was in for a real show.

Shelton was to do more than play guitar. Davis chose him to introduce him wherever they went. This was looked upon as heresy by old-time politicians, whose way had always been to have the candidate introduced by his local leader.

Davis had theorized that all of the leaders who didn't get to introduce the candidate would feel that they had been slighted, while no one could object to "one of the fellows in the band."

The campaign was terribly underfinanced. Just how broke they were can be attested to by the fact that Davis and Faser had to share a lower berth on the train ride from Shreveport to New Orleans on the old Southern Belle Line.

Davis began his campaign in Jonesboro and from there went to Rayville. World War II was raging, and Davis and Faser drove in an old Chevrolet. After fourteen flats they switched to a Buick donated by a car dealer supporter. Gas was also a problem, and much time was spent begging gas coupons.

In north Louisiana the crowds were immense, sometimes numbering five to ten thousand. South Louisiana was a different story. Davis recalls that his first south Louisiana meeting was in Carencro, and "counting the band and me, there were twenty-six people present."

This was soon alleviated by Davis' originating a fifteen-minute program at 7:00 A.M. from WJBO Radio in Baton Rouge. On the program he did a little speaking, and a lot of singing and ballyhooed his appearance schedule.

At no time in the campaign did Davis ever mention the opposition. In fact, he never even mentioned the word "opposition." He adhered to this throughout his political life.

What did he talk about? Well, first a trio from the band would sing. One favorite was *No Letter Today,* which oftentimes caused much weeping among the lady-folk in the crowd, all of whom had loved ones away at war. Other popular tunes were *It Makes No Difference Now* and *Worried Mind* and *Live and Let Live.*

In south Louisiana, where campaigning took place on Sundays, mostly in dancehalls, Cajun music such as *Big Mamou* and *Jolie Blonde* would be added to the program. Davis knew a song or two in French, which didn't hurt any.

The musical part of the program would always conclude with *You Are My Sunshine,* with everybody joining in. It was a tough act to follow.

Davis mostly spoke about peace and harmony. Louisiana had been ripped apart for generations by Long and anti-Long slugfests, and he promised to end that forever. He promised to bring all people together. It's amazing that beyond this, he made very few concrete promises!

The rest of his time was spent defending his singing, which by now had become a major target of the opposition. Davis would say to this, "They're raising Cain about my singing. I've never had regrets about me and my old guitar. It fed me when I was hungry and clothed me when I was ragged. If we had more singing and less fighting, we'd have a lot better world. If anybody in this crowd has ever seen anyone singing and fighting at the same time, I'd like him to raise his hand."

To capture the true flavor of a Jimmie Davis political speech, you must hear the man talk in his almost-halting, very low-keyed but very musical voice.

This passage comes closest to capturing the Davis way with words. The amazing fact is that these words were repeated over and over in a political campaign:

> I don't especially like to, but I must look to a
> time when they're going to take me, just like

they're going to take you, out to that silent city on a hill, where there are no big shots and no little shots—no rich men, no poor men—a place where six feet of earth make them all the same size. A place from whence no traveler returns, but a place from whence God's children will be borne away on the wings of heavenly angels to a beautiful home, not made with hands—with walls of jasper, gates of pearl, and streets of gold—in a garden of flowers that never fade.

The opposition was not exactly silent. A minor accusation was that Jimmie Davis didn't have enough experience to be governor. But the real thrust of their campaign was some risque records that Davis had written early in his career and recorded.

By today's standards the songs are extremely tame. Davis says, "They could even be played at some funerals!" But back then, the opposition felt it had dynamite.

The songs included *Bedbug Blues, Honky Tonk Blues, High-Geared Mama,* and *The Red Nightgown Blues.*

Circulars were distributed by the hundreds of thousands showing the actual phonograph record with the lyrics (in most cases highly doctored) printed below.

Congressman Jimmy Morrison ran a full-page ad in the Shreveport newspapers announcing an important message to be delivered at No Man's Land Park. He warned that only adults should hear this message and these records. He particularly invited ministers to be in attendance "at this historic event."

Davis gives this account of the Morrison rally. "On the speaker's platform, Morrison had set up a Victrola about as high as a giraffe. He started out playing my record of *The Red Nightgown Blues.* By the time he got to the first chorus, people were paired off and dancing all over the place. In no time at all there was no one left to hear the speaking. Morrison got mad, broke the record, and told the crowd, 'Elect him if you want him.' "

Nor was the wily Earl K. Long above attempting to take advantage of what he felt was Davis' main vulnerability. Long gathered a group of ministers from all over the state in a hotel room in New Orleans. There he put on a record of the *Bedbug Blues.*

While the record played, the preachers were very quiet. When the music stopped, someone exclaimed, "Praise the Lord; Jimmie Davis is a man who used to be on the wrong side of the fence, and now he's seen the light! Thank the Lord!"

Jimmie Davis was a very tough man to run against.

Still, his opponents tried. In liberal south Louisiana they portrayed Davis as a "blue-law man," someone who would interject his more conservative north Louisiana philosophy into their way of life. In north Louisiana Davis was pictured as a writer of dirty songs, "a honky-tonk man."

Davis kept right on singing and preaching the same "gospel"—"I'm not for or against the Longs; I want you to be a Davis man."

Davis heard the first-primary election returns in the Monteleone Hotel in New Orleans. Paper ballots were still in use in Louisiana, and it was late in the evening when he learned by radio that he had led Morgan by about fifty thousand votes. He had run poorly in New Orleans, well in south Louisiana, and "extremely well" in north Louisiana.

His ticket had not done as well and was running behind by approximately one hundred thousand votes. The Davis ticket included Emile Verret of New Iberia for lieutenant governor, Fred LeBlanc of Baton Rouge for attorney general, and Jim Gremillion of Crowley for secretary of state, and a few others.

The ticket, disheartened by its relatively poor showing, wanted to pull out of the race, but Davis implored them to stay in, explaining, "If I win by just eighteen thousand votes, we'll all go in."

Congressman Jimmy Morrison, who had run a close third behind Morgan, joined the second-place finisher against Davis with an endorsement.

The second primary got under way in earnest.

Davis remembers one event that happened during the campaign that he was never to forget. It was a political truism to which almost every man who has ever held public office can attest.

While on the campaign trail, Davis decided to pay a courtesy call on former Governor J. Y. Sanders, who had served Louisiana from 1912 to 1916 and who was now approaching ninety years of age. Sanders lived near Hammond.

Davis went to the door of the Sanders home and was greeted by Mrs. Sanders. He explained who he was and the purpose of his visit. Mrs. Sanders replied, "I'm glad to see you. If you hadn't come by, I was going to vote against you."

Governor Sanders entered, and the two men shook hands. Sanders said he thought Davis had a chance to win. They were served coffee, and as they sipped the dark brew from fine crystal cups, Sanders spoke: "Davis, I want to tell you this story.

"When I was elected to office, I was a young man. I was six feet, two inches tall, had never been sick a day in my life, was as strong as a bull, and could throw a cow down and milk her before she could get up. I could speak to crowds of ten thousand without a public address system and be heard on the back row. But, Davis, in two years' time I had become a stoop-shouldered old man. My friends got me . . . my friends got me."

Sanders' words lingered in Davis' ears as they drove away and for years to come.

The second primary was a duplicate of the first—same charges, same singing, and soft-spoken words.

Again election night was spent in New Orleans. Davis recalls having dinner that evening at Antoine's. "I wasn't worried about the results; I had done all that I could, and it was too late to change a thing." They finished dining at about 10:00 P.M. and still had no idea of the results.

Finally at campaign headquarters in the Monteleone Hotel, Davis heard that he'd been elected governor of Louisiana by about seventy-five thousand votes and had "even picked up some votes in New Orleans."

The sharecropper was now the governor of Louisiana.

11. *The First Term*

How does it feel to be elected governor of your state?

"Believe it or not, I wasn't all that excited. You know, when you put one hand on the Bible and the other up in the air and you say, 'I do, so help me God,' it suddenly dawns on you that you've got a wildcat by the tail, and you hope that you can do right by everyone, and you hope that your friends will stay with you."

The times in which he took office played a great role in the early years of that first Davis administration. In 1944 the war was still very much the dominant factor in the nation's life, and nothing, including a brand new governor, was unaffected.

Almost as soon as he took office, Davis was pressed into service by the federal government to headline bond rally shows across the nation. "There's no telling how many war bonds *You Are My Sunshine* sold." Not only did American audiences get top-notch country-and-Western music, but they got it performed by a governor! The combination seems to have gone well.

In November, 1944, the new governor and Alvern adopted a baby boy whom they named James William Davis. Everyone calls him "Jimmie." Davis recalls that the night they brought the baby to the mansion it was raining "cats and dogs."

"The weather was wet, Alvern's eyes were wet, my eyes were wet, and the baby was wet!"

Today, Jimmie farms in Newellton.

The life and death of any Louisiana governor is dependent to a large extent on his ability to get along with the state legislature. Davis took office with a legislature that had been, for the most part, opposed to his candidacy. In the unique wartime situation, this was not as serious as it might have been, because the fact of the matter was the war prohibited the legislature from doing almost anything.

When peace was declared a short time later, Davis called the legislature into special session, and the new administration really "got down to business."

As amazing as it may seem now, the State of Louisiana had no retirement system for its employees. The same held true for everyone connected with the educational system, from teachers to bus drivers to cafeteria workers. A person could spend his adult life working for the state in any capacity and, upon retirement, be turned out with perhaps a "thank you" and nothing else.

Under Davis, the legislature passed the state's first retirement system for those in education, not including teachers and the Louisiana Sheriff's department. Not only was this a just move, but it didn't hurt Davis' popularity any either.

The Davis administration then turned its attention to Louisiana's dying timber industry. Trees of all sizes were being cut down by the millions, and not one was being replanted. It was only a matter of time before the timber industry became an unhappy memory. Davis got the legislature to pass the state's first reforestation act, which provided for selective cutting and made mandatory the planting of new timber. The timber industry boomed, and tens of thousands of jobs were created for people who sorely needed work.

Davis then directed his efforts toward the millions of acres of Louisiana land that lay under water and were of no value or productivity to anyone but fish. Under Davis, a massive land reclamation program was begun, reclaiming millions of acres of rich earth from Louisiana's marshes and swamps.

A brand new college (now Nicholls State University) was built at Thibodaux, Louisiana, and the predominantly black Southern University at Baton Rouge was given its first infusion of new buildings in years. A new charity hospital was constructed in Shreveport, and the state's first driver's license law was enacted. Davis still has Louisiana Driver's License Number One!

Things were going well for the new governor, when he ran headlong into a reality that turns the fun of politics into cold nightmare. It was called "Right to Work," and it was to prove Governor Jimmie Davis' mettle.

A Right-to-Work Bill was introduced in the 1946 session of the legislature by a close friend of Davis', Senator William Cleveland of Crowley. "Right-to-Work" meant exactly what its name implies: a person could work on a job whether he was a union member or not, and there could be no picketing of a job.

This became the most emotional issue of its time; its residue still affects Louisiana politics, and a man's career can still be hurt or helped depending on how he voted on "Right-to-Work."

It was the hottest potato that a legislature could handle; for a governor it held much potential for quick political death.

The bill was passed by both houses of the legislature and then it went to the Governor to sign or veto.

The pressure on Davis was tremendous. The press was for the bill, the unions said it would mean the death of organized labor.

The singing had suddenly stopped for Jimmie H. Davis. He stood alone in a small and personal arena. It was decision time. Just his.

He vetoed the bill, and it is putting it mildly to say that all hell broke loose. The "peace and harmony" governor found himself in a war.

The most common accusation against Davis was that he had vetoed it because he himself was a member of the late James C. Petrillo's all-powerful musicians' union. Davis denies this. "I never was a member of any union; I didn't have the skill to belong. In my opinion, the bill as first proposed was not a bad one, but in its final form I felt it was too drastic."

Telegrams and letters poured into the Governor's Mansion in Baton Rouge. Some praised, most damned. A once-close friend sent this wire (with a copy to the newspapers):

"I'm sorry I ever knew you. I'm sorry I ever supported you. You've disgraced yourself, and you've disgraced Louisiana."

The telegram shook Davis, and he discussed it with Alvern. Alvern said, "For every piece of mail like that,

76

there are ten thousand people who wish you well. The average citizen is a lot more tolerant than that, and I believe people want you to do what you feel in your mind and heart is right."

Davis felt better.

Why did he veto it?

"I had already studied the thing from top to bottom and had sought the best advice on both sides of the question that was available at that time. We also knew that Florida had, a short time before, passed a similar piece of legislation that had been held by the courts to be unconstitutional. Furthermore, I thought it was too drastic. It was strictly my decision, and I made it alone."

Louisianians realized their governor was prepared to do more than sing pretty songs.

Despite the Right-to-Work explosion, Davis built and maintained excellent relations with the legislature and in fact ended each legislative session with the band at his side.

"I'd say, 'Gentlemen of the legislature, what's done is done.' Then I'd turn to the band and say, 'Give me a "G" chord, boys,' and I'd sing, *It Makes No Difference Now*."

And it really didn't!

While Davis was governor, the Democratic National Convention was held in Chicago, and the governor, as he traditionally does, led the Louisiana delegation.

At that convention two interesting things occurred—one best illustrates the kind of man Jimmie Davis was and is; the other was the beginning of a friendship between Louisiana's governor and the (for the moment) U.S. Senator from Missouri, Harry S Truman.

77

First, about Davis' character.

While at the convention in Chicago, Davis learned that New Orleans District Attorney Buddy Cocke had been elected district judge, thus creating a vacancy in the district attorney's office. At that time Louisiana's governor made almost every appointment to vacated offices which are now filled by election.

A group of prominent Louisiana citizens—headed by former Governor Sam H. Jones and including the late Congressman Hale Boggs, now U.S. Judge Robert Ainsworth, Jr., New Orleans Mayor Robert S. Maestri, and political leader Eva Talbot—joined the Governor and asked him to appoint Jimmy O'Connor (now a New Orleans judge) to the District Attorney's unexpired term. Davis responded that he was inclined to do what the group asked, but he refused to make a definite commitment, saying he wanted "to think about it a bit."

After the convention Davis was asked to come to a meeting in New Orleans with Leonard Nicholson, publisher of *The Times-Picayune,* and Ralph Nicholson, publisher and owner of the then New Orleans *Item.* Former Governor Jones and the group backing the O'Connor appointment (still unmade) were also asked to attend.

Jones began by saying they thought O'Connor would be a good district attorney. Leonard Nicholson got right to the point of the meeting. "Davis, if you appoint O'Connor D.A., we'll make you wish you'd never heard the word 'Governor'!"

Jones then allowed that perhaps they all ought to give the appointment more thought.

Jimmie Davis then spoke. As usual he spoke very quietly. He said, "Mr. Nicholson, I respect you as a newspaper man, but I think you should know I'm on my way to Baton Rouge now and without any further conversation. And when I get to my desk and can get hold of a fountain pen, you've got a brand new D.A. named Jimmy O'Connor."

It's interesting to note than when O'Connor later ran for a full term, it was with the endorsement of the New Orleans *Item*.

Back at the Democratic Convention in Chicago, the nomination for the Presidency was not in question. Franklin D. Roosevelt would be nominated for an unprecedented fourth term, and everyone knew it. What was in doubt was the fate of Roosevelt's vice president, Henry Wallace.

Davis was getting ready to leave the convention. Earlier he had led a hundred-piece band in the playing of *You Are My Sunshine*. Now he was about to catch a train to New York to conduct state business. Prior to his departure, he received a call from a St. Louis banker prominent in Democratic Party affairs. Would the Governor see Senator Harry S Truman in the Senator's suite at the Palmer House? Davis agreed to the meeting.

"Truman was obviously very nervous. He said he was on the spot and didn't want the vice-presidential nomination, but that if he didn't go for it, Henry Wallace might get it on the first ballot, and Wallace was just too liberal. He said he didn't have a single Southern vote, and he needed a Southerner to break the ice. Would I second his nomination? I cancelled my train reservation and did just that. He never forgot it and was always extremely kind."

In 1947 the Governor received an interesting offer. His agent, Mitch Hamilburg, and a movie director named Lindsay Parsons came to Baton Rouge and asked him if

79

he'd star in a motion picture about his own life. The picture was to be called *Louisiana*.

Davis said he had "a vacation coming," and he took off for twelve days to go to Hollywood, where all of the interior shots were done on the Monogram Pictures lot. Outside locations were shot in Louisiana and included much of north Louisiana, Louisiana College in Pineville, Dodd College for Women, Louisiana State University, the State Capitol in Baton Rouge, and the New Orleans French Quarter.

Davis says that the role was "easy, I just had to be myself." He feels that the picture was amazingly accurate. Alvern was portrayed by Margaret Lindsay.

It was, one might venture, an unusual experience, even for a governor. *Louisiana* still turns up regularly on the late show.

Nor was Davis neglecting his recording. He would fly to Nashville or New York—depending on where the recording session was—on a Saturday afternoon, record that night, and be back in the governor's office on Monday morning.

"Most of the time no one knew the difference, except of course the lieutenant governor, who has to be informed when the governor leaves the state.

"I had become established in the recording business with a lifetime contract and I didn't intend to give it up as long as I could do this without taking any time from my official duties. And I did it without taking one hour of the state's time."

Jimmie and the band were also playing a tremendous number of benefits around the state. Jimmie says, "A time or two I tried just to speak, but they just wouldn't have it. So the band was brought along every place."

As Jimmie's term in office drew to a close, he took

80

satisfaction in several accomplishments. Despite his veto of the Right-to-Work Bill, he had mended the fences with most legislators. More important, he left the state a balanced budget, and without additional taxes, and with a tremendous surplus in the state treasury.

The entire senate signed a resolution praising Davis for a job well done, and then all sang *You Are My Sunshine.*

Jimmie Davis was Citizen Davis again.

12. *The Years Between*

That Jimmie Davis was pleased to be out of the governor's office is a major understatement. "I really hadn't relaxed in four years. It even affected my stomach, and the entire time I was governor I subsisted on goat's milk, vanilla wafers, and pea soup. I knew I needed some time to put the pieces back together."

Jimmie determined that the best way to do this was to accept an offer to make a vaudeville tour of the country. He would play the major cities for one-week stands and the smaller ones for two or three days. There would be three to five shows a day.

In addition to Jimmie and a seven-piece band, the show included a comedian and a girl singer.

While playing Washington's National Theatre, Jimmie had a couple of experiences that he likes to tell.

One night he got a telephone call from his old friend, now the President of the United States, Harry S Truman. Truman invited Jimmie to come and have lunch the next day at the White House. Jimmie protested that the President was too busy, but Truman was insistent, and the next day a White House limousine was waiting to take him to the President.

"The whole family was there—Harry, Bess, and Margaret. Before we sat down to lunch, the President sat down at the piano and played a couple of tunes which I gathered relaxed him. They were the *Missouri Waltz* and *Let Me Call You Sweetheart*."

Davis found the President almost despondent. Truman said, "I didn't want this blankety-blank job. It's killing Bess. If I can get close to Westbrook Pegler for what he's been writing about Margaret's singing, I'm going to bust him right in the face. My enemies say she's terrible, my friends say she's great. I don't know enough about music to really know what the hell she's doing, but I do know that if I get near Pegler, he's in for a fight."

Davis reports that he had occasion to visit the President again some six months later and found Truman's attitude toward the presidency completely changed.

Harry S Truman said, "It's a pretty fascinating job!"

While performing in Washington, Jimmie noticed a young couple on the front row at every performance. "We were playing five a day for a full week, and they were there every single show. Finally, the last night my curiosity couldn't take it any more, and I questioned them from the stage. 'What are you folks doing here?' I asked. The young man replied from his seat, 'We've been trying to figure out just what in the hell youall are trying to do!' I almost fainted; then the man busted out laughing and explained that he and his wife were on their honeymoon and loved country music and had

The Years Between

decided to see every show. 'When the shows are over, so is the honeymoon,' he explained."

One night Jimmie was singing in a dance hall in Texas when he had an experience that was to shape his show business endeavors for all time. A young soldier in uniform came up and asked if he could have a seat.

He had a glass in his hand, and it was obvious that he had been drinking pretty heavily. I told him to have a seat, and we chatted for fifteen minutes, but I could see he had something on his mind. He said, "I'm drunk now, but I didn't always drink. I came from a fine home and had good raising."

I didn't say anything. It was obvious he needed someone to listen. I thought he was going to tell me about himself, and I almost fell out of my chair when he proceeded to talk about me.

The soldier said, "I don't think this is the kind of place where a man who's been honored by the people of his state should be performing, even though I know it's just a profession to you. It seems to me that a man like you should be an inspiration to people. I know this is strange advice to come from a twenty-one-year-old soldier, and I wouldn't even be offering it if I wasn't full of whiskey."

It was time for me to perform again, and I thanked the boy. Then I made my way through this large crowd and up onto the bandstand. I asked the crowd to come closer and told them I had an announcement to make. When they had all gathered around, I said, "This will be the last song that Jimmie Davis will ever sing in a dance hall. It's not that I'm all that good, but perhaps I've got some other things to do with my life.' I sang the old hymn, *Lord, I'm Coming Home* and they all joined in—such singing you've never heard. The soldier was right in front with tears falling like rain. I said, 'Thank you and good night.'

"When I was through singing, I looked for the soldier to thank him for setting me straight, but he was gone. I never even knew his name. If he happens to read this book, I want him to write or call me.

Back in Shreveport, Jimmie settled down to "playing a few dates here and there, making a picture or two, writing some music, and doing some recording."

He also undertook one of the most successful and sustained radio shows in history, "The Jimmie Davis Hour," which was syndicated to thirteen states for some eight years.

The show was taped in Nashville, and Jimmie's group included Owen Bradley on the piano, the Anita Kerr singers, Grady Martin on guitar, and occasionally a fellow named Chet Atkins, plus three or four other band members.

The show was sponsored by two of Davis' lifelong friends, W. L. "Buddy" Billups of Hammond (Billups Petroleum Co.) and L. C. Latham of Rose Oil Company.

In addition to the financial considerations, "which were excellent," the show kept the Davis name alive in Louisiana. He may not have been in the Governor's Mansion any more, but he was in just about everybody's home in the state. "Out of sight, out of mind" didn't apply to the former governor!

In 1952, Davis recorded two of his most famous gospel numbers, *Suppertime* and *Mansion Over the Hilltop*. A short time later he wrote a song that was to become a classic, *Someone to Care*.

Perhaps it's well to examine exactly how the song came to be written and then to have a look at the words, which are reflective of Davis' faith and his ability to communicate with total simplicity.

> I badly needed a rest, and a couple of friends, Lindsay Coit and Lamar Loe, suggested that I use their hunting and fishing camp in the woods out from Newellton. I was totally alone. When the sun went down, you'd had it, and night would bring the sounds of hoot owls, whippoorwills, wolves, crickets, and katydids. I decided to do my own cooking, and I soon found out I wasn't a cook. The single meal I cooked lasted me for five days! Out there alone, you have a chance to reflect, to think, oh, about a lot of things, and out of this thinking I had the urge to express myself in poetry and music. The words and the tune came at the same time, and I wrote them in a night or two.

When the world seems cold and your friends seem few,
There is someone who cares for you;
When you've tears in your eyes,
Your heart bleeds inside,
There is someone who cares for you:
Chorus:
Someone to care, someone to share
All your troubles like no other can do;
He'll come down from the skies and
brush the tears from your eyes,
You're His child and He cares for you.

Davis says, "The music gave me great comfort. It's a way out of a problem. When I grow a little weary, as we all do, I turn to singing. It's never let me down."

Along with music, Davis had always been an avid hunter and fisherman, and whenever he could, he slipped away for both. Experts say he is brilliant with a rifle or a fly rod. He has the trophies to prove it. He particularly enjoys Louisiana quail hunting, and he belongs to a duck-hunting club in south Louisiana. He also hunted deer in Texas and moose and bear in Alaska.

During his time out of office, there was one thing he did avoid meticulously, and that was politics. Occasionally he went to Baton Rouge and had lunch at the mansion with whoever occupied it at the time. But he carefully avoided any participation whatever in the bloody campaigns.

He was able to do this until 1959, when people from all over the state began to flock to Shreveport and talk about something that Jimmie didn't want to hear: one more campaign for the governor's office.

Jimmie's parents with grandpa and grandma Davis.
Jimmie is sitting in grandma's lap.

Jimmie at age 5.

Grandma Davis at 94 years old.

Beech Springs
Elementary School.
Arrow points
to Jimmie Davis.

Beech Springs basketball team. Ball is between Jimmie's feet.

The old Davis home place.

Left: Jimmie getting ready for college.

Below: Graduation day at L.S.U.

On the day of Jimmie's wedding to Alvern Adams at her home in Shreveport.

Jimmie with his band, the Anita Kerr Singers, and Owen Bradley at the Organ.

Jimmie in a night club scene from the motion picture, "Strictly in the Groove."

Looking at some
of his mail that came in at
radio station KWKH
during his early years as a
country singer.

4832-10

As Jimmie appeared in the movie "Mississippi Rhythm."

Left to right: Captain Humphrey, Police Chief Grady Williamson,
Police Commissioner Jimmie Davis, Captain Kent.

Tossing his hat into the ring for the governorship of Louisiana.

On the campaign trail.

A strategy session in New Orleans.

Left to right: Judge Robert A. Ainsworth (now judge of the Federal Court of Appeals),
Jesse Davis (Jimmie's brother), Owen Brennan, Jimmie Davis,
Judge James P. O'Connor, and "Slim" Harbert (a member of the Davis band).

Actors and actresses playing the part of the Davis family in the movie "Louisiana."

Another scene from the movie "Louisiana" showing mother and father Davis putting the children to bed.

Mrs. Davis
with the two head chefs
at the Governor's Mansion.

Jimmie being sworn in as governor at his first inauguration by Supreme Court Justice O'Neill.

Tex Ritter pays a visit to Jimmie.

With a life-long friend, Red Foley.

Left to right: Dr. Gabriel Ackal, Paul Harvey, Governor Davis, and Leslie Farrow.

Jack Dempsey showing his fists to Jimmie Davis.

...mmie, flanked on left by Jimmy Wakely of western movies,
...d on right by Gene Austin, author of "My Blue Heaven."

Lawrence Welk visits Jimmie at his home.

Jimmie Davis with Gene Autry.

From a New Orleans scene
with Margaret Lindsay
who played the part of Mrs. Davis
in "Louisiana."

People lined up for blocks to see the premiere showing of "Louisiana."

"My son, Jim, had just asked me
'Dad, why did you want to give up all that good hunting and fishing
and get into a mess like this?
I said, 'Jim, just a minute—I'm getting ready to speak
and then I'll tell you.'

...king the oath of office in 1960. Supreme Court Justice Joe B. Hamiter presides.

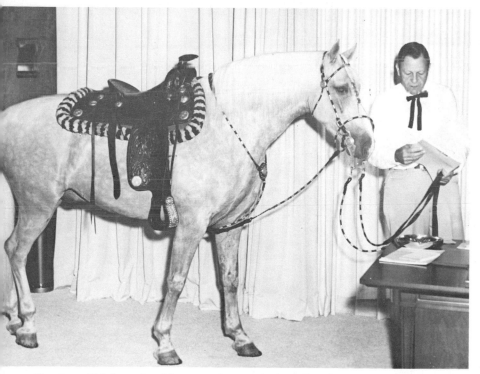

Jimmie and his horse Sunshine open the morning's mail at the governor's office.

Former President John F. Kennedy, Governor Jimmie Davi
and mayor Victor Schiro of New Orleans. "It was a few days late
that President Kennedy was killed in the same car in which we were riding," Jimmie say

Mrs. Harriet Quinn with Anna and Jimmie Davis.
Jimmie says, "The Lord never made a finer cook than Harriet."

The Governor's Mansion at Baton Rouge, Louisiana. It was built during Jimmie's
second administration.

Jimmie, Jr., shoots his first deer at eleven years of age.

Autographing albums at a Florida concert are: James, Anna, and Jimmie Davis.

The Jimmie Davis camp on Toledo Bend Lake.

The Jimmie Davis trio as they appear today: Jimmie, Anna Davis, and James Wilson.

Western star Johnny Mack Brown with Jimmie.

Minnie Pearl with Jimmie and Anna.

Jimmie and his wife, Anna, flanked by Eddie and Barbara Miller. Eddie is the writer of "Release Me."

Jimmie and Marijohn Wilkins with the Jordanaires.

Jimmie Davis receiving the Manny Award from Ralph Emery at the Nashville Songwriters' Association.

Jimmie Davis with Tanya Tucker.

**With the king
of the Bluegrass,
Bill Monroe.**

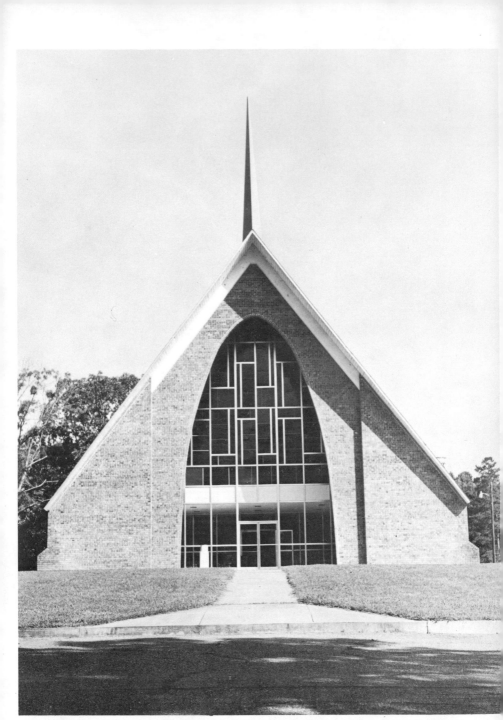

The Jimmie Davis Tabernacle—located between Jonesboro and Quitman, Louisiana.

13. *Another Run for the Roses*

The year 1959 found Davis satisfied with life. "I was doing all right." In any other state he would have probably gone on just that way, "doing all right." But Louisiana wasn't any other state; it was a state standing on a hilltop and sniffing the air, because that "time" had come —the time to elect a brand-new governor.

It was then, as it is today, the time that most Louisianians really live for.

People from all walks of life and from every economic strata began to descend on Davis in Shreveport. Their question was always the same: Wouldn't he consider one more try?

Davis thought not. "I never had been married to politics and made it a point never to get addicted to it either. I had long ago observed that when a man's out of office and trying desperately to get back in, he's a frustrated and unhappy man. I really didn't want to mess up my life."

He did discuss it with Alvern. "She left it entirely up to me. I guess she knew as well as I did the headaches and the heartaches, and she didn't try to encourage or discourage me. She said, 'I just want you to be happy.' "

When the pressure to run became so great that it could no longer be ignored, Davis called his old friend Chris Faser, who was now living in Mississippi where he had been elected to that state's legislature twice.

Just how remarkable a politician Faser was (and is) can be attested to by his getting elected to the legislatures of both Mississippi and Louisiana in a relatively brief span of time! Perhaps someone else has accomplished that, but no record of it could be found.

Davis and Faser met in New Orleans. Faser had announced for re-election and didn't have any opposition, but his decision was immediate. "Governor, I think you can win, and I'll resign from the legislature this week and be there on Monday to help out."

Davis asked Faser to "hold up a day or two," as he still wanted to discuss the race with other members of his family.

"We were a very close family. We really loved each other, and I presented the political situation to them as honestly as I knew how. One sister said, 'Don't run, because if you're elected you not only create problems for yourself but for the whole family. I'm tired of people asking me why Jimmie did this or didn't do that, when really I don't know scat about it. I care for you as much as a sister can for her brother, but I think I'll buy television time and tell why I think you shouldn't be elected.' "

Davis replied, "I won't think less of you if you do just that, because that's the way it's supposed to be—everybody expressing himself or herself and voting for whom he pleases. I won't worry about it for one minute, but what I would worry about is if the day should come—and God pity us if it ever does—when you wouldn't have the privilege of going to the ballot box and voting exactly for whom you please."

The family's consternation—and, for that matter, Davis' own—was totally understandable. The next governor, whoever he would be, would face the most critical years in the history of Louisiana since the Civil War.

The years 1960 to 1964 would witness a legal and bloody clash between state and federal government over the issue of segregation.

This single, highly emotional issue would divide the state, pitting husband against wife, brother against brother, north against south, and race against race.

In retrospect it is amazing that anyone wanted to be governor at all. But when qualifying for that office had come and gone, the name Jimmie H. Davis was right among a whole lot of others.

Early opinion polls showed New Orleans Mayor De-Lesseps S. Morrison an easy front-runner. There was no doubt in any candidate's mind that it would be the urbane and sophisticated mayor whom he would have to face in a second primary. The job was to get into that second primary.

Conversely, it was felt that in a second primary, almost any candidate, especially Davis, could defeat Morrison, whose vote going in was made up of the mayor's tremendous New Orleans following, and many south Louisianians who, like Morrison, were Catholic.

Some of the other candidates, in addition to Davis and Morrison, were no less colorful. They included William J. Dodd, a former Earl K. Long lieutenant governor and then state comptroller; State Senator Willie Rainach, a prominent figure in the Citizen's Council movement in the South; and James A. Noe, a Monroe, Louisiana, millionaire who had served as governor for a brief time. Noe was the Long candidate and could boast of incumbent governor Earl K. Long (who under the then-existing state constitution could not seek re-election as an incumbent) as a candidate for lieutenant governor.

Long's inclusion on the ticket immediately assured Louisiana's "politics-lovin' " citizenry of an all-out, knock-down-and-drag-out campaign. They were not to be disappointed.

All candidates, including the liberal Morrison, espoused segregation. They did it in degrees, with Senator Rainach not only making the issue dominant in his own campaign, but bringing it to the forefront of everyone else's. It is interesting to note that exactly twelve years later, no man can hardly be elected governor of Louisiana without the black vote. But that wasn't the way it was back then.

With Rainach fanning the flames, the cry of the day became massive resistance at the ballot box to pending federal action that would destroy segregation in Louisiana forever.

Jimmie Davis, never an issue candidate, ran a typical Davis campaign that shrewdly placed him right in the center between the far right Rainach forces and the more liberal Morrison faction. Jimmie felt that in the middle was where most Louisianians were, and the Beech Springs troubadour was right on target.

What Davis didn't know was that he would be everyone else's target. The rallying cry of all other candidates was to "keep Jimmie out of the second primary." The means taken to accomplish this are way out even for Louisiana's unique politics.

116

Jimmie and Faser with band and quartet hit the road seriously. In Homer, Rainach's home town, Davis ran into a crowd that wasn't exactly anxious to hear him speak or sing. Schools had been let out, and the hand of every child held a Rainach banner. Every time Davis tried to speak, there were cries of "Rainach!" Davis decided to praise his opponent, and this quieted the crowd enough for Jimmie to get a word or two in. It was a harrowing experience, and Homer wasn't scheduled too often thereafter.

At about this time the strategy—if it can be called that—that would be used against Davis was developed.

At least three of his opponents, independently of one another, sent detectives to California (scene of Davis' movie and recording ventures) to "get the goods on Jimmie."

Davis says the place was overrun with Louisiana detectives all looking into him. Among the accusations that would come out of those trips were that Davis had been arrested for drunk driving; that Davis had owned and operated a night club in Palm Springs, California, that was integrated; that Davis was wanted for bank robbery; and that he had operated a whiskey still in New Hampshire.

As Davis says, "They found fifty-seven Jimmie Davises in California who had gotten into some kind of scrape with the law, and they brought back all of their photographs and fingerprints. They even found some who slightly resembled me. It was one whale of an experience for a man who has never even gotten a parking ticket in all his life."

Jimmie just thought he'd seen what was coming. One candidate for governor (now a close friend of Davis') acknowledged that he paid a New York photographer some eight thousand dollars to make a false, composite photograph showing Davis dancing with Lena Horne in a California nightspot. This photo is a legend in Louisiana politics. Given the times and the mood of the citizenry, the picture exploded like dynamite in Louisiana.

Today Davis can laugh about it. "I've never met the lady, and she's never met me. I've seen her in the movies and on television, and she's obviously a great artist and a fine person. But no, we never danced."

Louisianians weren't so sure, and candidate William J. "Bill" Dodd, a brilliant man and public speaker, took every opportunity to publicly discuss the matter. Dodd felt that he had to defeat Davis to get into the second primary. His problem was the eternal problem faced by anyone opposing Davis: he was seldom there in person or issue to oppose.

"I knew I had to draw him out somehow, make him deny the accusations, do anything to get him to stop singing and start talking," says Dodd.

Dodd chose the community of Holly Ridge in north Louisiana to "give it a whirl."

All candidates had been invited to speak, and Davis said he wouldn't be there, explaining to his leadership, "I'll just draw the others a crowd." But the leadership prevailed, and against his better judgment, Jimmie showed up at Holly Ridge.

"I saw Dodd's face light up when he saw me drive in, and I told Chris, 'Oh, oh, I'm in for it.' Did he forever tear me up! I was a drunk driver, a nightclub owner, a bank robber, and a moonshiner, and there I was in that photograph (dropped to the crowd from an airplane) dancing with Lena Horne."

The crowd, in Davis country, began to boo Dodd.

Dodd recalls telling a lieutenant, "I've got him now; he's got to answer me on all of that!"

118

They really didn't know Jimmie Davis yet.

Now Davis walked slowly to the platform, and the boos changed to cheers. They loved "ole Jimmie." Davis said, "You've already heard my life story. You know all about me by this time, and there's not too much I can add to it other than to sing you a song or two. So gather 'round, friends."

Dodd says the Davis performance was "astonishing." "He just took all that criticism and never gave it back, so it never went any further. He simply could not be suckered into anyone else's ball game. He knew that issues were secondary to personalities in Louisiana politics. And there in Holly Ridge, he sprinkled them with *You Are My Sunshine,* he took them home to *Suppertime,* and then nailed me to *The Old Rugged Cross.* I was running against a brilliant phantom."

On another occasion Davis was campaigning in northwest Louisiana. He and his entourage arrived at noon with the rally scheduled for a vacant lot at 1:00 P.M. Davis recalls, "People had already started gathering."

The group of men, including Davis, Chris Faser, Ed Reed and Charles Mitchell decided to have lunch in the town's only cafe. They chose a corner table and Davis sat facing the wall.

As they ordered one of Davis' opponents henchman came in carrying the highly derogatory anti-Davis circulars. Not seeing the men at the corner table he proceeded to hand a circular to a redheaded waitress who appeared to be about twenty-three years old.

The henchman said, "Young lady, I know you're going to vote for somebody for Governor, but don't vote for this Jimmie Davis. Read this circular and you'll find out that he's sold bootleg whiskey, he's robbed several banks, and he's written these terrible songs."

The waitress replied, "You get out of here! I don't care

if he wrote *The Cathouse Blues,* I'm for Jimmie Davis!"

The effectiveness of the Davis "method" is perhaps best illustrated by what happened at Ferriday, Louisiana. The big issue was a proposed stock law which the people opposed because the law would require the building of fences to contain the cattle on a person's own pasture rather than letting the cattle run free out on the open range. Davis was giving his usual speech when someone in the audience yelled out, "Where do you stand on this stock law issue?"

Jimmie says, "I stopped what I was saying, turned to the band, and requested an A chord. Then I sang that old Western number, *Don't Fence Me In,* then went right on with my speech."

Davis' campaign manager I. W. "Pat" Patterson was in St. Landry Parish (county), the largest parish in Louisiana in percentage of black voters. Patterson went to see another legendary figure, Sheriff Cat Doucet, to try to make a "deal" for the black vote, which was then to some extent a controlled vote that could be delivered "to the right party."

Patterson asked the sheriff what it would cost. The sheriff wasn't sure. "Maybe ten, maybe twelve thousand dollars." Patterson said, "That's out of line. I'll give you six thousand dollars—three thousand in cash and three thousand in escrow if you'll deliver those votes."

The sheriff looked puzzled. "That fellow 'escrow'—he's on our side?"

The first primary went about as expected, with Morrison leading by approximately seventy thousand votes. Davis ran second. The one surprise was Rainach's strong third-place finish, which indicated that people felt a lot stronger on the segregation issue than most anticipated.

The incumbent Governor Earl K. Long finished third in the race for lieutenant governor, and some said Longism was finished in Louisiana.

In the second primary Morrison tried desperately what others had tried before him—to get Jimmie Davis to "come on out, to be substantive enough to take apart."

Morrison challenged Davis to a debate on television, and when Davis did not reply, Morrison went on television alone, with an empty chair and a guitar on it and a sign reading "Jimmie Davis." To this Davis replied, "There's no use in me debating Morrison because I'm voting for Jimmie Davis and he can't change my mind."

Support from many diverse quarters soon came to Davis. He was endorsed by Earl Long, Rainach, and the New Orleans *Times–Picayune!* Morrison could not get over it and asked, "Isn't this a fine jambalaya—with Earl Long, the *Times–Picayune*, Leander Perez, the *Shreveport Times* . . . the old regulars . . . this all together in one pot . . . a mixture that the entire history of Louisiana has never seen before?"

It was a mixture that would never be seen again.

The attack against Morrison was simple and direct: he was "soft" on integration and was the "NAACP candidate."

Morrison fought back, saying, "I've been sued by the NAACP more often than any other official in the state."

The attempt by Morrison to create a strong segregationist image failed, and Davis cut deeply into Morrison's first-primary vote, defeating the New Orleans mayor by seventy thousand votes.

As with almost every other political opponent, Davis and Morrison were personally good friends. Davis had supported Morrison in at least one of the Mayor's successful bids for office. A few days before Morrison's ill-fated flight which resulted in his death he dined with Davis in the Davis's home.

At any rate, the sharecropper was once more to occupy the Governor's Mansion of Louisiana.

What kind of politician was Jimmie Davis? For that matter, was he a politician at all? Perhaps William J. "Bill" Dodd summed him up best: "Davis was a professional politician as well as a professional artist. Skin Earl Long and Jimmie Davis and lay them on the ground and you couldn't tell them apart. They just had a different exterior, a difference of styles. They had the same objectives, the same background, many of the same expressions, and many of the same friends. If Earl wanted to get back at someone, he wanted to make a show of it. Davis fired you, and you left thanking him and feeling appreciative. You were still fired! I guess the difference was, politics wasn't Jimmie Davis' whole life. And strangely, amazingly, the office pursued Davis more than he pursued it."

14. *The Second Term*

At high noon on a sweltering Tuesday, the first of May of 1960, Jimmie Davis raised his right hand and took the oath for governor for a second time while the bells in a nearby church steeple tolled.

If anybody thought it was hot that day, they hadn't seen anything yet! A war was in its earliest stages—a war between what white Southerners called "our way of life" and the federal government, which had determined to make Louisiana the test state in its assault on school segregation.

The battle lines were unmistakable: a white population that almost to the man wanted to maintain the way things had always been and a federal court system poised to sweep away any act that it felt was impeding integration of the public school system.

Pressure applied to those elected to public office was at a fever pitch. The public wanted "something done."

Any official who stood in the way of that massive feeling stood a good chance of impeachment or worse.

Jimmie Davis, the peace-and-harmony man, the singer of hymns, and the speaker of soft words, found himself the commander-in-chief of an army that could in a moment turn into a mob capable of anything.

Davis saw his mission as threefold: to avoid bloodshed, to keep the public schools open, and to test in the courts every law on the books pertaining to segregation.

Amazingly, he succeeded at all three.

Equally amazing is the fact that in the final analysis he had little to do with maintaining or stopping integration or Negro voter registration. As Professors Henry C. Dethloff and Allen E. Begnaud of the University of Southwestern Louisiana point out, "The matter was out of his hands."

The state's vocal conservative forces were led by Judge Leander Perez of Plaquemines Parish, a brilliant attorney and one of the fathers of the White Citizens Council movement in the South. Perez did not lack for lieutenants, as many north Louisiana legislators, as well as the lieutenant governor and the attorney general, joined to stop what could not be stopped.

The day Davis took office, the Legislature convened and "segregation bills and resolutions hit the hopper on every conceivable angle pertaining to the issue."

These bills were passed automatically and signed into law. Just that quickly, the courts declared them unconstitutional and the process would begin all over again.

In that first year five special sessions in a row were called on the same subject: segregation.

Their work turned out to be largely meaningless except for one very important aspect: these sessions did give the raging citizenry an outlet for emotions—at least something tangible, something that they could see and hear,

124

was being done. These sessions may have helped to prevent bloodshed.

Davis was being served federal subpoenas on a daily basis.

Just how strong was the feeling for segregation by the white majority? Perhaps these examples tell the story:

The Legislature passed a concurrent resolution instructing Davis to send a delegation to see the newly elected (but not yet inaugurated) President of the United States, John F. Kennedy.

Chris Faser and a group of legislators went to Palm Beach, Florida, to meet with the President. They never got to see him. Instead, they explained Louisiana's case to then-presidential advisor Clark Clifford.

Faser says that Clifford listened politely and said little. "I had the feeling he thought we were all crazy."

On another occasion conservative forces tried to pressure Davis into sending an army consisting of National Guard troops and the state police to Mississippi to help that state keep James Meredith out of Ole Miss.

Davis responded, "We better tend to our own business."

Another time it was strongly "suggested" to Davis that he commission armed men to go "with guns" to New Orleans "to throw out the Orleans Parish school system and take over the schools and run them."

Davis says, "We didn't do it."

It's a fair question to ask what would have happened to Jimmie Davis if he had completely "stood up" to the Legislature. The answer is ridiculously simple: he would have been impeached that day.

Just how rough this period of Louisiana's history was can be attested to by an article appearing in the Baton Rouge Sunday Advocate of July 11, 1976:

In the Jimmie Davis administration of 1960–

125

1964, legislators were bombarded with mail, telephone calls, and visits from constituents, asking for their representatives and senators to oppose integration.

The public was not prepared to accept sex education or racial integration in the 60s. Neither was the public prepared to accept a right-to-work measure in the mid 1950s (or else organized labor convinced legislators so), for after having right-to-work for two years, the legislature repealed the measure.

On November 5, 1963, in a statewide television address, Davis summed up what had transpired in this way: "Today, looking back, I believe the record will show that we did what had to be done, and it was done within the framework of law and order. We closed no schools. We lost no lives. We shed no blood. Let those who would find fault with our efforts compare them with some of our sister states who were, perhaps, not as fortunate."

In 1929, Huey P. Long, serving his first term as Louisiana's governor, announced that he could no longer live in the existing Governor's Mansion. His explanation was both simple and unique: there were too many rats in the place and there were too many clocks. To this list, termites were later added.

With one hundred fifty thousand dollars from the state's Board of Liquidation and the Governor leading a gang of convicts from the state penitentiary, the old mansion was torn down and a new one erected.

The outcry from the state's more conservative elements and the press was ferocious but did not seem to bother the Kingfish.

Louisiana history, perhaps like all history, has a strange

way of repeating itself, and midway in Jimmie Davis'
second term in office, Alvern and Commissioner of Administration James Reily voiced the feelings that Louisiana needed a modern Governor's Mansion.

Jimmie describes what was wrong with the existing
mansion this way: "The radiators sounded like the Civil
War; every morning you thought you were at the Battle of
Gettysburg. Whether you wanted to or not, you got up.
When there was a bad rain, the roof leaked. We knew we
needed something better. We discussed it and decided
to build the most imposing Governor's Mansion in the
United States—one that would not only house the governor and his family and all of the official entertaining
that you have to do, but one that would be a major tourist attraction. We did just that!"

It wasn't quite that easy. When legislation was introduced appropriating money for the construction, the
matter was hotly contested. Opponents felt that Louisiana
could do a lot more with its money than build a governor's mansion, but the bill passed by a small margin, and
a million dollars was appropriated.

Perhaps Davis' reaction to the hue and cry against a
new mansion is an interesting glimpse into the Jimmie
Davis philosophy of leadership.

> I'd have preferred that everybody had been for
> the mansion, but everybody wouldn't have been for
> it if the Lord had come down here and delivered
> it in a big truck!
>
> If you've got to wait for everybody to be for
> something, you might as well go on home. If you've
> got to get everybody's approval on any state project,
> you wouldn't have your first highway, your first
> bridge, the first school building, the first hospital,
> or the first anything!

If you believe it's good, go with it. If you don't,
leave it alone.

Today the mansion is acknowledged to be this nation's
finest and is a major tourist attraction gathering thousands to Baton Rouge day in and day out. Architect William C. Gilmer of Shreveport gives much of the credit
for the Mansion's usability to Alvern.

He points out that as the Davises were in the executive
mansion for a second term, "Mrs. Davis certainly had a
working knowledge of what was necessary for the life and
entertaining of the state and what had been lacking or
limited in the existing mansion."

The mansion is of modified Louisiana Greek-revival
style and is situated high on a knoll overlooking three
small lakes behind the State Capitol. The four-level
building is lined with twenty-one white Doric columns.
From thirty-branch crystal chandeliers dating from the
1830s to hand-woven Oriental rugs with scenes depicting
highlights of Louisiana history in border vignettes, the
Mansion is indeed something to see.

How much does Davis like it?

Jimmie and his wife reside in a home on the lake directly by the side of the mansion. Its very first occupant
can always keep an eye on it.

Among the most controversial projects of the Davis
administration was the Sunshine Bridge, which pretty
well answers Shakespeare's question, "What's in a name?"

If the name happens to be "Sunshine" and the state
happens to be Louisiana and Jimmie Davis happens to
be Governor, the answer is "plenty!"

Davis felt that a bridge was needed across the Mississippi River halfway between New Orleans and Baton Rouge—a distance of eighty miles.

"We couldn't get industry to locate on the west side of the river until we had a bridge. We were lagging terribly behind other Southern states in industrial development." Davis said this bridge would mean much to the state's economy and to the convenience of its people, and would be much safer than a ferry boat.

The bridge cost some thirty million dollars. Today the cost would be a hundred million dollars.

Critics said the bridge began nowhere and ended nowhere. Davis feels that the real storm arose over the bridge's name. Louisiana law holds that no public structure can be named after a living person. Davis' political enemies felt that "The Sunshine Bridge" was just another way of saying "The Jimmie Davis Bridge."

A reporter asked Davis why the bridge had been given that name. Davis responded, "I think it's because the sun rises in the East and sets in the West."

How does he feel about the bridge's name today?

"We had to name it something. If we'd called it 'The Heavenly Bridge' or 'The Road to Damascus,' someone wouldn't have liked it."

A lot less controversial was the Davis-built bridge between Baton Rouge and Port Allen, just across the Mississippi from each other. It should be noted, however, that this bridge also had its opponents.

Despite the tremendous outpouring of money and energy on the segregation issue, the second Davis administration was not without some tangible and lasting accomplishments.

The most important of these to Jimmie personally was Act 561 of the 1960 Legislature. This act was, without a doubt, the single most important piece of legislation dealing with mental retardation ever passed in Louisiana up to that time.

The act provided for the first time a comprehensive approach to the problem—an approach that brought into play and coordinated all of the state's resources and agencies. Davis quickly moved to give this legislation "teeth" by pouring more than nine million dollars into new facilities, including three new residential schools for retarded children.

That same act created nine day-care centers throughout the state which provided for the needs of trainable and educable retarded children through evaluation, education, and rehabilitation.

In recognition of his work in this field, Davis was the recipient of the President's Cup as the Louisiana citizen who had contributed most to helping the retarded.

Nor was the state's desperately needed industrial development program neglected. Louisiana needed industry for jobs for its citizenry, and from 1960 to 1964, more than three quarters of a billion dollars was invested in the state, creating more than sixteen thousand jobs.

Under Davis' leadership, the states of Louisiana and Texas joined in the huge Toledo Bend Dam project, which provided for the construction of a sixty-million-dollar hydroelectric plant and dam on the Sabine River. The immense Toledo Bend reservoir furnished power, navigational facilities, and water for industrial processes, as well as recreational facilities for the whole south-central United States.

Perhaps the project's most unique feature, considering the times, was that it was financed by the two states involved without federal funds.

Davis also built the Earl K. Long Charity Hospital at

Baton Rouge, which closed the final gap in the state's charity hospital program and provided heavily populated Baton Rouge with a much-needed major medical facility.

While the 1960–64 period may have been both grim and full of fury, it must also be noted that the times were not without moments of levity, to a great extent fostered by the Jimmie Davis brand of humor.

In the first year of Davis' second term, the Governor acquired a magnificent horse, part quarter horse and part Arabian. Davis purchased the animal from a man named Mexican Pete who lived on Lake St. John near Jonesville. He promptly named the three-year-old animal . . . what else . . . "Sunshine."

The horse with the Governor in the saddle became famous and appeared in all of the major bowl parades except the Rose Bowl.

Jimmie says the horse "was a true ham, loved parades, bands and people, and was very gentle with children."

Jimmie Davis loved that horse.

One day Jimmie and some members of the press were sitting in the Governor's office. Sunshine was outside, all saddled up for an event later that morning.

A member of the press asked the Governor about Sunshine. Jimmie replied, "Just a minute." He then went outside, mounted Sunshine, and rode him up the Capitol steps and into the governor's office!

Davis says cameramen were following "closely behind, hoping for an accident." One of them was carrying a wash tub. There was no accident because, Davis claims, "Sunshine was just too smart."

A member of the press asked Davis why he'd done it. Davis' response was direct: "Sunshine had never been in the governor's office before."

One reporter noted that "that was the first time the whole horse was ever in the governor's office."

Sunshine is buried on the Davis farm at Newellton. There is a monument over the grave which bears Sunshine's picture.

Government is facts and figures, cold statistics of black ink and red ink. So overwhelming are these compilations that it is all too easy to lose sight that government must also deal with people, very often desperate people to whom government is indeed a court of last resort.

Jimmie Davis talks about these people.

> Some days it's nothing but sadness, it's as if all the world's misery comes calling at your door. I've seen old women, stooped with age, plead for a son who is in the penitentiary. I've had fathers sit at my desk with their heads buried in their hands and weep for some child gone wrong. Sometimes you can help. Sometimes the law says that you can't.
>
> I recall so vividly one winter day when a poorly dressed woman accompanied by five small children, three of them barefooted, came to see me about her husband and the children's father who was serving time in the pen as a first offender. The children were crying and the three youngest obviously had colds. I silently wished that I was someplace else and that the Lieutenant Governor was sitting behind my desk.
>
> In the midst of all the tears the youngest child, a girl of about four left her mother's arms and walked over to my desk. She looked up at me and said, "Governor, do you have a little girl?" I said, "No I don't, but I wish I had one like you." Then as she climbed up on my lap she asked if I had "a little boy?" I said, "Yes, I have one about your

size." Let me tell you I wet the top of her head with my own tears.

I looked at them for a moment and I said, "The Pardon Board meets a week from this coming Monday. I want all of you to go there dressed exactly as you are today and without a lawyer. Tell them the story you just told me and be sure to emphasize that this is your husband's first offense. Perhaps they'll vote to let him out on probation or even pardon him. Then they'll send it to me for my approval or disapproval. I'm telling you this because I as Governor am powerless to act either way until I have a recommendation from the Pardon Board."

About ten days later it was my pleasure to reunite this family just in time for Christmas. I managed to keep up with the case and the man straightened up and made a good citizen.

Surely one Louisiana legislative session ended in a manner unique even for a state in which the unique was practically the norm. It was nearing midnight, the time when the session would by law end *sine die.*

The Senate was in recess waiting for the House to act on a resolution so that it could hurriedly act on it prior to adjournment. The resolution was one that Chris Faser didn't particularly want to see pass into law. But what could he do? He was only one man.

The House did pass the resolution, and it was given to a clerk to carry quickly to the Senate. When the clerk passed through the Capitol rotunda which separates the two legislative branches, Faser asked him if he could see the measure for a moment. The man passed the legislation to Faser, who quickly disappeared into the crowd with it.

There was a mad and frantic search to find the lost resolution. As midnight approached, Faser, along with

Assistant Highway Director George Dupuis, returned quietly to the Senate, where a legislator was lambasting the loss of the measure.

On Faser's signal, Dupis turned off the lights in the Legislature while Faser turned off all of the microphones. Suddenly the angry senator found himself not only in darkness but speaking into a dead mike.

The session ended in a pandemonium unusual even for Louisiana!

While at LSU working on his master's degree, Davis felt that one certain professor was not being fair to him. In the Jimmie Davis manner, he said nothing about it. But he waited.

Years later when Davis was governor, the professor was serving as chairman of a national conference in Baton Rouge. He asked if he could use the House chamber for the conference. Davis said, "Of course." He then asked the Governor if he would address the conference, which would be comprised of professional people. Davis said, "Definitely."

When the time came for Davis to step from the Governor's office to the House chamber to deliver his welcoming message, he sent instead a legislator who was known for two qualities: he liked his toddy, and he loved to talk about past battles in the war, in which he claimed to have been a participant.

The legislator, with a bottle in his back pocket, stood before the convention and spoke. Naturally he spoke about his old favorite stories.

The audience sat dumbstruck as the speech lengthened into thirty minutes, then an hour, and an hour and a half. After two hours Davis sent the substitute speaker word to quit, and the convention ended forever.

134

15. *In Sickness and in Health . . . Till Death Do Us Part*

In 1962, in the magnificent Governor's Mansion in Baton Rouge, a scene occurred that has occurred and can occur any place.

Alvern detected a lump in her breast. She said, "This is different. I have a suspicion that this is it."

Surgery was performed. There was a malignancy, and it was removed. As she was coming out of the anesthetic, Alvern asked Jimmie, "Did they get it all?" He replied, "Yes, they said they got it; they're happy with the results." The couple looked at each other for a moment, and Alvern dropped off to sleep.

For two years the disease slumbered, and Alvern and Jimmie went to Houston for Alvern's checkup. The diagnosis was chilling: cancer in both lungs. "She was far too bright to hide the facts from, and she was the kind of person who wanted to know. She asked the doctor, 'How much time have I got?' He replied, 'Well, maybe a couple of years.' "

Alvern wept. It was the first time that Jimmie Davis had ever seen his wife cry about this. "I held on; it was tough, because the Lord knows I wanted to let go. I tried to encourage her, but what could I say? We took the long ride home to Baton Rouge. We tried to make small talk, tried to act normal, but both of us were crushed inside."

For a brief time they were able to live normally, but then Alvern's spine and both lungs collapsed. She remained at home for a while and then went to the hospital, where she was fitted for a brace so that she could hold up her head. Her spine could no longer support it.

At the hospital, Alvern told Jimmie, "I've got to exercise some way. I want to sit up." Jimmie replied that the doctor wouldn't permit it. Alvern said, "Lock the door." Jimmie helped her up for half a minute and the next day for a full minute. After a time she could sit up for a while, and her doctor still didn't know it.

Alvern Adams Davis decided that she wanted to stand, and Jimmie and Magnolia Jones, their maid and cook, helped her until finally she could stand alone. One day the doctors were astonished to see Alvern being wheeled in a chair by Jimmie down the long hospital hall.

It seemed to be a miracle. Her lungs and spine appeared to have healed, and Alvern went downtown to shop and even attended meetings of the Louisiana State University Board of Supervisors, of which she was a member.

And then "it hit her again," and she returned home to bed and to nurses around the clock. Jimmie says he slept "with one eye open; she could have hemorrhaged at any time."

One morning her doctor felt her pulse and told Jimmie that they had better get Alvern back to the hospital. "She may have a couple of days."

"The day she left our home was the second time I ever saw Alvern cry," Jimmie says. "She knew she would never come back."

A few minutes before Alvern passed away, Mrs. Spears, a nurse, entered to give her a shot. Alvern was totally lucid. "No," she said, "I don't need it, I feel fine. Let's have a race." Mrs. Spears asked, "What kind of race?" "A foot race," said Alvern, who hadn't walked in nearly two years.

Then she said to Jimmie, "I wish you could see what I see now. Such a beautiful sight as you could never imagine. I hope some day you'll see it."

Alvern asked to speak to Jimmie, Jr., alone, and Jimmie stepped out of the room. "I don't know what she told him, and I never asked. That was between mother and son.

"When I came back into the room, peace was on her face and pain had left her. She was passing on to that great beyond that she had hoped for for so long. There's a heaven, and I know she's there. Alvern kept me going.

"If I had been the greatest infidel on earth and had not been a believer in God, my opinion of God and the hereafter would have been completely changed after watching her die. She was happier at death's door than most people are in a lifetime."

After Alvern's passing, her mother, Mrs. W. M. Adams, moved in with Jimmie, and the two shared their grief.

16. *Tabernacle*

Prior to the end of Jimmie's second term as governor, a long-time Davis friend—W. L. "Buddy" Billups, a Hammond, Louisiana, millionaire and philanthropist—suggested that Davis' unique career be noted and honored in some enduring way.

Billups suggested "a tabernacle, a non-denominational house of worship especially equipped to house musical events."

Davis agreed and chose for the site some fourteen acres of ground, which he donated, on the old Beech Springs school grounds in Jackson Parish. Land for the edifice was cleared and landscaped by James P. Cross of New Iberia and Clyde Blalock of Jonesboro.

Close to half a million dollars was raised by a one-hundred-dollar-a-plate testimonial dinner and by donations from friends, supporters, and gospel music lovers.

The edifice was dedicated on May 16, 1965, with some five thousand well-wishers eating twenty-two hundred pounds of roast pig, then moving inside to hear speeches and singing by the Plainsmen Quartet, the Happy Goodman Family, the Dixie Echoes, the Florida Boys, choirs from churches throughout the area, and of course Jimmie himself, who led the singing of *Amazing Grace* to get the program underway.

The Baton Rouge *Morning Advocate* noted that "five crying babies" were present for the ceremonies. There was also about fifteen minutes of rain, which didn't deter anyone.

Davis, not given to adjective, has called the tabernacle "the most beautiful country church in the world."

It may be. It rests atop a modest hill—an impressive brick structure which features a sharply elevated roof containing an oval arch. The entire triangular peak, which is topped by a steeple, has windows of purple glass. The melodic chimes contained within can be heard by residents for miles around.

Inside, large laminated beams, with curvature resembling that of the exterior, emphasize the tabernacle's spaciousness. Total seating capacity is eight hundred. The interior also features rich panelings, lime oak pews, and an ornamental baptistry. The building is air conditioned and has both a piano and an organ; the sound system, even by Jimmie Davis' standards, is perfect.

An eight-hundred-foot well, located outside, feeds a lovely water fountain.

Also located on the grounds is the tiny, log-cabin Peckerwood Hill Store, offering souvenirs, soft drinks, and a look at relics from a bygone day. Beside its porch is the old-fashioned water well, complete with wooden bucket and tin dipper and wash bowl on its frame. Mounted on the wall nearby is a small mirror and a towel on a rusty nail. Around the corner near the side entrance hangs a mop and a washtub, and on the steps a covered crock.

Flanked on the left of the tabernacle in the distance is the once-used old homeplace of Davis' parents: weather-beaten, clean, scrubbed. Here, too, is a wide porch, water well, and its accessories. There is a neat heap of firewood on the porch.

Inside, the basic necessities of another day have been preserved: the old family trunk, the grandfather clock, the well-worn Bible and picture album, the stark iron bedstead, a wooden table and wooden chairs, a wood-burning stove in the kitchen, and a mantle laden with bygone necessities—salve, liniment, quinine, turpentine.

The tabernacle is used by church groups, schools, and singing groups. Each year Jimmie returns for a "Homecoming Day," when he and Anna, state dignitaries, and several quartets recall another time in music and word.

Alvern Davis is buried behind the tabernacle, near the old Davis home. The inscription on her grave reads: "Alvern Adams Davis, 1906–1967, loving wife of Governor Jimmie Davis. She was the daughter of Dr. and Mrs. W. M. Adams."

In front of the tabernacle is a sundial donated by the people of the community. Its motto reads: "Count only the sunny hours."

17. *A Lady Named Anna*

As Jimmie Davis toured the United States, appearing at gospel concerts in almost every state, his path often crossed that of The Chuck Wagon Gang, one of the most beloved groups and vital forces in gospel music for over twenty-five years.

The group, a family quartet, had started out in their home town of Lubbock, Texas, led by D. P. (Dad) Carter. They had been on radio and traveled the dusty byways to perform in storefronts, schools, churches, anywhere there was an audience. Soon they became a watchword in the gospel field. In 1935, they began to record for Columbia Records and became one of the most popular gospel groups in America.

After D. P. Carter passed away, the group kept right on, and even today their records are consistent best-sellers for Columbia.

The foursome consisted of Rose, Roy, Eddie, and

Anna, whose husband had passed away some two years before in 1966.

Here's how Anna described what she knew about fellow performer Jimmie Davis: "To the people in the gospel field, Jimmie was special. We all admired him and were a little in awe of him. I remember how my sister Rose and I would always stay for his numbers even when we should have been getting ready for our own."

Jimmie had known Anna's late husband, as well as her father and brother. Jimmie's wife and Anna's husband had passed away at just about the same time. One night Jimmie went along with a group of friends to dinner in Nashville. Included in the group was the lovely Anna.

It was in no way a date because Anna's young son wouldn't let his mother have any dates! "My son didn't approve of anyone until Jimmie Davis came along. I was proud that he felt that way."

Jimmie Davis up close surprised her. "He was so down to earth, and we had so much in common, most of all just about the same background. I found him handsome, too!"

The couple began to date, and Jimmie says, "We didn't need a lot of talk. Both of us were mind readers, and we knew how we felt."

Davis' story of the proposal and the wedding are classics of the Davis-type humor.

"I proposed on the telephone. Those long-distance calls couldn't go on. Anna was afraid to accept because she wasn't sure I had the money. She said she'd try to help me make a living!"

In December, 1969, the couple went to Ringgold, Georgia, about twenty miles from Chattanooga, Tennessee, to get married. They drove with Jimmie, Anna, her son, Greg, and the preacher, Buck Rambo, his wife

Dottie and their daughter Reba all in the car. Jimmie says, "We weren't taking any chances on losing the preacher."

Jimmie says he went "incognito," wearing a coat that he could barely see out of. First they located the town clerk, a lady.

> We explained our mission, and she told us to have a seat. Then a man rushed in and said he had lost his peace officer's commission and he was afraid he couldn't arrest anyone. She told him to have a seat. At that time a lady came in and said she couldn't find her marriage license and was it all right for her children? She asked, "Am I married now or not?" The clerk invited her to wait her turn.
>
> Finally they got to me. Asked my occupation and I said, "Farmer." A man standing against a wall said, "You sing some, too, don't you?" I said, "No, sir, you've got me confused with my father." He introduced himself as the judge and said he'd heard me sing several times. I asked him, "Judge, can you get us into a church?" He said he'd call and have one opened up. Then we asked if they knew where we could get a photographer for the occasion. They said they knew one lady who owned a camera, but she hadn't learned to use it yet. We said that would be fine, and when the lady with the camera arrived, we all worked on it to try to get it to work. The thing exploded, and in the one picture we got, we all came out looking like a bunch of kangaroos in a free-for-all fight.
>
> After the ceremony I spotted a cafe and invited the Judge to join us for a wedding dinner. We got hot dogs and soda pop, and I believe one or two got hamburgers. The bill came to $1.89, and with a

tip, exactly two dollars. I hadn't planned to spend quite that much, but I paid cheerfully.

After the $1.89 dinner, Jimmie and Anna went to New York for their honeymoon.

The Jimmie–Anna marriage has turned out to be a wonderful one, and everybody who knows them says that Anna is one of the two best "things" that ever happened to Jimmie Davis.

18. *The Last Campaign*

In early 1971, Jimmie Davis became the recipient of a pressure he neither sought nor wanted. Friends who had been out of the power and the limelight that go with being close to the governor of the state "wanted back in."

Davis says, "I had nothing to gain; I'd been there twice. Anna and I had a wonderful life. The one thing I didn't need was the unbelievable pressure of the governor's office."

Davis was not alone in this sentiment. "I'm from a large family, and at heart they were all against my running again. Anna, who'd never been any place close to politics before, was dead set against it, too."

Davis promised his friends he'd "look into it." He really didn't. The Davis way, tried and proven, would have been to "hit the campaign trail" about a year in advance, buying a couple of dollars of gasoline here, stopping in for coffee there, meeting people, shaking hands, talking about the crops, and inquiring about the children.

Davis says, "I just couldn't bring myself to do it."

Thus the all-important year of advance work never got underway, though the pressure to run intensified. By the time the decision was made to seek office, the die had been cast—the election was too close at hand.

This may not have been true for other politicians. For Jimmie Davis, who had his own "way to go about it," it was very true.

As other candidates began to qualify for governor, something else that all but spelled defeat also emerged: Jimmie Davis' traditional, politically strong geographic areas were each producing their own candidates, in some cases more than one.

Out of Shreveport itself, Davis' home base, came state senator—and now U.S. Senator—J. Bennett Johnston. In central Louisiana, U.S. Representative Gillis W. Long of Alexandria announced, and in northeast Louisiana, U.S. Representative Speedy O. Long of Jena and State Highway Board member James Moore of Monroe threw their hats into the ring.

The worst blow to Davis' chances came when his former lieutenant governor, C. C. "Taddy" Aycock of Franklin, announced that he too was a candidate. Aycock was perhaps closer than any man (in the public mind) to the Jimmie Davis political philosophy. Davis felt that while he might be able to weather the geographic splits in his vote, it would be almost impossible to overcome a philosophic division, too.

He talked with Aycock on two occasions in an attempt to get the incumbent lieutenant governor to withdraw.

"I asked him to stop by my house if he was ever in Baton Rouge, and one day he came by. I said, 'Taddy, I think you'll make a mistake in running, and as it's looking now, I may be making a mistake in doing it. I'm confident I'll get more votes than you will. If you'd consider running for lieutenant governor on my ticket, I don't think we'd have any trouble winning.' "

Aycock said, "There's no way I can do that. I'm going to run for governor, mainly for my family. They say I've always been a bridesmaid but never a bride."

Davis said, "I understand, and we'll always be friends. When I spoke in south Louisiana, I suppose I often said more good things about Taddy Aycock than I said about myself."

The author has spoken to five people who were with Davis on election night. All five give the same report. As the returns came in showing that Davis would not win, everyone present noticed the same thing: a look of great relief on the face of Jimmie Davis.

Anna Davis said that night, "If you don't mind, I could shout all the way to the Capitol!"

Davis replied, "Don't mind? I'll shout with you. Let's go!"

Davis now adds to this, "And we lived happily ever after." He also remembers what his father said when he first discussed with him the possibility of seeking public office: "The only thing worse than losing is winning."

Davis has become good friends with his next-door neighbor, Governor Edwin Edwards, now serving a second term. He feels that he and Edwards have one important thing in common: "We're both the sons of sharecroppers."

19. *And Still Another Career!*

There's a secret to Jimmie Davis' eternal youth: the man doesn't stop. His energy and enthusiasm would tire a boy; his willingness to move on to other things even when he doesn't have to is an amazing phenomenon to witness.

By 1973, he had achieved enough for at least three lifetimes. He had been elected to public office countless times, he had composed some of the world's most beloved sacred and country-and-Western music, and he was considered a box-office draw in just about every state in the nation. His records were selling well, and he was booked for all of the gospel concerts where he cared to perform.

And then he got a telephone call that was to add still another facet to a remarkable career. Reverend John Ramsey, pastor of Rolling Hills Baptist Church, in Fort Worth, Texas, was on the phone inquiring if Jimmie could come to Fort Worth. Davis asked, "You mean to sing?" The Reverend replied, "To sing and speak at my morning service." Jimmie considered the unusual request for a moment and then gave his answer. "I won't preach, but I will speak as a layman to laymen." Reverend Ramsey said that would be fine, and a new career was born.

Davis set out to write his speech. He felt he had much he wanted to say. He had seen a lot of life and lived a lot of life and had done both from the depths of poverty and the heights of power. He felt that his unique view of the way things were and just where man was in all of that might have meaning for others, and he was anxious to share his experience and his vision.

Davis admits that that initial speech wasn't going too well. A seasoned performer, he sensed that his audience was not with him. He did all that he knew how to do. He put down his manuscript and spoke from his heart.

"It was immediately okay."

In the congregation was Dr. R. J. Barber of Danville, Virginia, who called Jimmie a few days later and asked him to sing and speak at his church.

Out of the Davis–Danville relationship has come an unusual agreement. The church has requested an annual visit from Jimmie Davis as long as he lives!

Today, Jimmie is in demand in pulpits across the nation and is now booked two years ahead.

In a typical year his speaking engagements took him to Spartanburg, South Carolina; Fort Worth, Texas; Lexington, Kentucky; Dallas, Texas; Lakeland, Florida; Tuscaloosa, Alabama; Richardson, Texas; Danville, Virginia; Shreveport, Louisiana; Savannah, Georgia; Tyler, Texas; Alexandria, Louisiana; Meridian, Mississippi; Arcadia, Louisiana; Baltimore, Maryland; Louisville, Kentucky; Miami, Florida; and Kingsport, Tennessee.

And Still Another Career!

And these do not include his gospel-singing engagements!

Jimmie is accompanied by Anna, who in some areas is as well known as he is through her work with The Chuck Wagon Gang. Both Anna and Jimmie love to travel. Also along is James Wilson of Center, Texas, who sings with Davis on many of his records and has also worked with The Chuck Wagon Gang on tours.

Typically, Jimmie will try to fly up the Saturday before the Sunday service so that he can do a bit of rehearsing with the church choir. He finds working with local choirs "mutually satisfying."

At the 11:00 A.M. service on Sunday, Davis begins by singing a couple of his own classics such as *Someone to Care* and *Suppertime.* Then he gives his speech. Some of his titles are "Chickens Come Home to Roost," "Today's Answer," "The Prodigal Son," and "The Great Homecoming."

The Davis style of speaking is exactly like the man: soft-spoken, easygoing. There is no shouting. A "rip-roaring" presentation would be as foreign to him as his speaking in Chinese. Nor does he try to compete with the preacher. He is what he is: a layman speaking to other laymen.

After the morning service, Davis is usually honored by dignitaries ranging from the host state's governor to U.S. senators to the local mayor. Often he is presented the key to the city.

This is followed by lunch on the grounds with the preacher and his guests.

After lunch, Jimmie and Anna return to their motel for rest. Davis begins the evening service with the songs he's rehearsed with the choir. These may be *Three Nails,*

153

How Great Thou Art, or *The Eastern Gate.* Then the choir joins the rest of the congregation, and Jimmie presents a half-hour concert of sacred music.

Anna and Jimmie return to their Baton Rouge home by air the following morning if weather permits.

A logical question to ask Davis, now that he has spoken from so many pulpits, is: Does he have any second thoughts about never having gone into the ministry?

He says no and feels that perhaps he can draw into church some people with whom the preacher might have difficulty. The experience has given him an almost awesome respect for preachers.

He says, "The more churches I visit, the more I realize and the more I appreciate these men who give so much to the salvation of others and who ask so little in return."

You can tell that this new phase of his life means a great deal to him. "Most people have never talked to a governor, and a lot of people come through curiosity. I try to get acquainted with the people from the pulpit and, in this getting-acquainted process, let them know that my life hasn't been much different from theirs. If there's a difference, it would be that I came up under perhaps poorer circumstances than almost anybody in the building.

"I let them know that I'm not there as a clergyman, but rather like the rest of the fellows sitting out there in the congregation. Once I'm able to establish that, I hope that I'm able to shed some little light on this sometimes frightening experience of human existence. Hopefully, even a bit of comfort."

20. *Presidents and Minstrels*

As a governor and entertainer, Jimmie Davis has met with almost everybody who is anybody in the United States. While he appears to have liked them all, you do get the impression that he wasn't as impressed with them as he was with the members of that Beech Springs basketball team that almost won the district rally so many years ago.

Davis is just not the impressionable type, with the possible exception of President Harry S Truman, whom Davis rates "our greatest."

Davis loved the man's practicality and "down-home" approach to everything. "Truman knew people, and he was a great student of all that he didn't know. He consulted on everything, but he called the shots."

The first time Davis saw Franklin D. Roosevelt was during Roosevelt's first try at the presidency. Jimmie was in New York on a recording date and out of curiosity went to Madison Square Garden to hear the young man from Hyde Park speak. Even then he was conscious of presidential security and recalls at least one hundred fifty mounted New York policemen controlling the crowds outside the Garden and three hundred fifty officers inside.

When Davis was Governor, he and the senator from Missouri were staying at the Mayflower Hotel in Washington. The two began to chat, and Truman asked if Davis would like to have dinner at the White House. He and Truman walked there (and back) and had dinner with President and Mrs. Roosevelt.

"Roosevelt's knowledge of Louisiana was unbelievable. He knew about every problem we had. I recall his asking specifically about various industries in the New Orleans and Lake Charles areas. Mrs. Roosevelt was most gracious; the atmosphere was completely relaxed."

Once when Governor and Mrs. Davis were vacationing at Camp Pendleton Marine Base near Oceanside, California, Jimmie learned that the President was also there for swimming and therapy. The two managed to chat as Roosevelt was carried from the pool for a massage.

"I was shocked how the disease had ravaged this handsome man's thighs and legs. It was a pitiful sight, and if anyone doesn't believe that Roosevelt carried a great burden, he should have been at that poolside.

"I didn't agree with everything Roosevelt did, and I'm sure he didn't agree with everything I did. He was the President, and somebody's got to call the game."

Governor Davis visited President Dwight D. Eisenhower in the President's office. "He was a military man, and it showed. There were no wasted words, no small talk. He was gracious, but not a man you could really relax with."

156

Davis remembers President John F. Kennedy as "a charming man, very bright, with a great sense of humor, if a somewhat salty one."

Jimmie visited the President in Washington to discuss the settlement of Louisiana's tremendous tidelands claim against the United States government.

"I had occasional back trouble, as he did, and I admired his rocking chair. The President invited me to try it, and I did. He asked me if I liked it, and I told him it was awfully comfortable. 'I'll send you one,' Kennedy promised, and sure enough, three weeks later a rocker bearing a small plaque arrived."

As Davis dictated this biography (1976), the rocker sat a few feet from his hand.

There's a bit of John F. Kennedy in Baton Rouge, Louisiana.

A short time later the President came to New Orleans on a speaking engagement. The presidential limousine (the same one he rode in on that fateful Dallas trip) was flown down, and the President, Governor Davis, and the then New Orleans Mayor Victor Schiro rode together.

"There were thousands upon thousands of people along the way," Davis recalls, "and the FBI later said one Lee Harvey Oswald was among them. Then, just a face in the crowd. A short time later the President was assassinated."

Davis accepts the Warren Commission Report and believes that Oswald was the lone killer of the President even though others may have known about the plans. "But that's just my opinion."

Davis knew President Lyndon Johnson quite well. They had met on many occasions in Louisiana, Texas, and Florida when Johnson was seeking the Democratic vice-presidential nomination and, prior to that, when Johnson was Democratic leader in the Senate.

"We could communicate quite easily. He was from Texas, and I was from near Shreveport. He knew a lot about Louisiana and even owned a television station in Lafayette. He appeared to be a good man, but I never had the occasion to test him."

Jimmie remembers Richard M. Nixon as a vivacious, hard working man whom he believes to be the best public relations man this country ever had.

"I was sorry, of course, about his misfortune and I doubt if I know any more about exactly what happened than the average person does who reads this book. And naturally, I would not be in a position to comment.

"Although his wife, Pat, seemed to make it a point not to have too much to say in connection with the president's business, but from what I saw of the family, she was more interested in his welfare and success than any other person in the nation. Her charm and politeness to all people is beyond description."

Jimmie Davis is very difficult to interview on other entertainers. You just can't get him to talk badly about another performer. He explains, "It's an awfully tough game."

In a lifetime of "playing that game," Davis has worked with the greats and the less-than-greats.

Davis recalls once being in Richardson's Music Store in Shreveport talking to the clerk, Louise McCauley, who also filled in as his accompanist sometimes on KWKH.

"A young recording artist came in dressed in the loudest cowboy outfit we'd ever seen. His belt buckle alone was the size of the top of a steel drum. As he was walking out, Louise said, 'He thinks he's going to be a star!' I said, 'He might be; you can never tell.' "

The loudly dressed cowboy was Gene Autry, and later he and Davis became great friends, with Davis visiting him many times on the set at Republic Pictures where Autry reigned as king.

When Davis finished his film biography, *Louisiana,* Autry gave him a party.

Davis describes Autry as "a principled man, a real good American."

Governor Davis was on a bond-selling tour in Alabama, and Governor Jim Folsom invited him to the governor's mansion "to meet his new wife."

"A young fellow was brought in with his guitar to entertain us, and we all sang together," Davis recalls. "This young fellow began to sing some of his own compositions, and I felt like a ton of bricks had hit my head. I thought, 'He's got it!' "

The young fellow was Hank Williams, and he and Davis became close friends and collaborators on two or three compositions.

> He was a great poet and had a style all of his own. When he came to Shreveport to play on the Louisiana Hayride, we'd have him out to lunch. He was already touched by tragedy, and it was written all over him. He had a bad back and tried to kill the pain with whatever he could.
>
> Once I flew to Nashville to visit him and do some writing with him. He and Hank, Jr., met me at the airport in a big Cadillac. As he was backing out, we rammed into someone's Chevrolet. Hank refused to sign the insurance form accepting responsibility, and the police came. It was obvious that

159

Hank would be put in jail, and I begged him to sign the release, which he finally did. I insisted on driving. He was just in no condition.

Hank and I stayed up until two-thirty in the morning, and when I went to bed, he was still sitting there with his guitar in his hand, paper around him on the floor. I hate to say it, but he could create better when he wasn't himself. It was as if he occupied some magic world all of his own.

The best number we wrote that night he lost— never did find it. The next day he sent his band off to fill an engagement. He just couldn't make it. Hank Williams was a tragedy in every sense of the word.

One night in Shreveport, Davis needed another guitarist quickly to fill an engagement in West Monroe. Finally he located a young fellow just making his start on the Louisiana Hayride.

"I paid him forty dollars for the show, but I don't think I could hire him for that now."

The "fill-in" guitarist was Elvis Presley!

Davis, a good friend of Presley and his manager Colonel Tom Parker, says that Elvis is a "nice, well-mannered young fellow, but he could drive them crazy even back then!"

Once, on a network radio show from California, Davis and an up-and-going singer sang a duet of *You Are My Sunshine*. The other half of the duet was Frank Sinatra, whom Davis describes as a real pro. "He's a perfectionist and a natural, a take-charge artist who knows exactly what he wants and who gets it."

Jimmie recalls one Decca recording session in which he and the other artists sat around waiting their turn. The others were Bing Crosby, Ella Fitzgerald, and Jimmy and Tommy Dorsey.

Davis says Crosby was a quiet, almost moody man who could occasionally be very jovial. Here's how Jimmie describes the recording session at which Crosby recorded Davis' song *Nobody's Darling But Mine:*

"Bing showed up about four hours late. He walked in, sat on a high stool in front of a mike, and asked somebody to give him the song. He read it over and asked the band to play it once. Then he said, 'Let's make it.' He did four or five numbers that way."

Once Davis was at a Decca recording session in New York. It was one of his first and he was very nervous, but obviously not as nervous as a young lady who sat waiting her turn.

"She was so obviously shook that I told her to relax, everything would be fine. She thanked me and we introduced ourselves."

The young lady was Mary Martin.

Ed Sullivan was another friend of Jimmie's. Jimmie met him when, along with Bob Gilmore of Southern Music Company, they attended the World's Fair held in New York. Then, Sullivan was a newspaper columnist. Later he invited Jimmie on two occasions to appear on his television show, but Jimmie felt that, as Governor, he couldn't.

Of the old-timers, Davis thought Ted Lewis "a wonderful entertainer," and he could still spend all night listening to the Mills Brothers.

He considers Wayne Newton perhaps the best in the business today, and always enjoyed Dinah Shore as an all 'round artist—one of the best in the entertainment field.

21. *Letters*

Over the years, Jimmie Davis has received, both as governor and entertainer, letters that can only be described as astonishing. No dream, no scheme, no hope, and no despair has not been commented on in the correspondence that has poured in to Jimmie Davis.

We've included just a sample of these letters. They'll make you laugh. They'll make you cry, too.

Laplace, Louisiana: I was wonderin' if there wasn't a little dead head job you could give me? I know plenty of people have had such jobs.

Evanston, Illinois: I have known for the last two presidential elections that I should probably be elected president or marry Adlai Stevenson and let him be elected, but I was still married to my x-husband and even if he is a lawyer he could not run for president and it has been one thing after another. I am a virgin and I have two small children to support and I am 38 years old.

Bastrop, Louisiana: Since I am a Christian I do not hunt on Sunday. I only have two weeks vacation each year and in the past I have taken one week in the spring for fishing and one in the fall for hunting. My request is, Sir, to exceed the bag limit to make up for the Sunday I do not hunt.

Houston, Texas: Dear Governor Davis, let me ask you a question. How come you are able to live in a heavenly world here on earth? With me the day I arrived on earth from my mother's womb the devil been after me with poverty and despair.

Abbeville, Louisiana: I need this information *quick.* If it is possible I would like to know if
white male, is or has ever been married. Hurry!

Pineville, Louisiana: Please have the wrestling matches investigated for brutality. I have been witnessing matches on Lafayette TV and I think there has been some of the most outrageous brutality, not fit for humans to view.

Reserve, Louisiana: Just a few words to let you know our next door neighbor is mad with us. To tease us he has 19 deer dogs, five cats and some fighting roosters. They crow all day. I can't stand that no more.

Durant, Oklahoma: I know you through your songs and I love to hear you sing. This morning it was *Did You Ever Think to Pray?* I am just an old old lady who is going home to heaven pretty soon and I mean to talk with the Lord Jesus about you when I get there.

Pennsylvania (with photo): Here I am in a grass hula skirt at Ocean City, N.J. about fifteen years ago. I have no current.

Oak Ridge, Louisiana: I have heard different stories about the welfare and would like to have your opinion

164

on them. They say that a woman cannot have sexual relations with a man when she is on welfare. Do you think a woman is going to let her nature kill her just to draw a check? Please help me cause I've got to know something!

Bogalusa, Louisiana: The mill where my husband works is on strike and he and I are bringing in seventeen dollars a week. We could not have made it without your records. I love the woods, moonlight and rain and sun and the strike cannot take that.

Lumberton, Mississippi: Please for the sake of people like me, make records and leave politics to others that can't sing.

New Orleans, Louisiana: I am a young "petite" brunette prostitute. I am not proud of my profession, but seem to have been destined for this "dirty" work. Now I am sick. A welfare worker told me she could arrange it so I could draw one hundred dollars per month if I'd give up my profession. I told her I could make that much in an hour, when able to work.

Memphis, Tennessee: Recently my grandmother came to spend the winter with our family. She is good, country stock and a true Christian. To see that 87 year old lady sit and listen to you singing with tears running down her cheeks truly is heart rending.

DeRidder, Louisiana: I am a little boy 8 years old. I am in the third grade. I have 2 dogs a big dog and a little dog—I like to hear you sing and I like dogs.

Gulfport, Mississippi: I am an ex-drunkard and am working with drunkards trying to find the peace that I have. You have been a great spiritual blessing to me

165

through your singing. I could not have made it without you.

Sulphur, Louisiana: I want the chiropractor to stay in business because he is the only one that could cure my heel.

Houston, Texas: Please help me. Here are my problems. My girlfriend is underage. Second, she feels that she is unclean because two years ago she lived in a nightmare and third, she has cancer. But I love her.

Des Moines, Iowa: About three years ago I had an emotional breakdown. It seemed that I could hardly face the day as I would wake up in the morning. Then I got your record *Someone to Care.* It told me something I desperately needed to know—someone cared about me.

New Orleans, Louisiana: I received a letter from the state that I was dead but I am not dead! I'm alive as a young guinea. So send my welfare check.

Baton Rouge, Louisiana: I noticed that the new Governor's Mansion will soon be finished and I guess you will be moving in. I was just wondering what you are going to do with the old one. I would appreciate it very much if you would loan it to me and my family.

Marmaduke, Arkansas: I truly believe that your religious recordings played a big part in my being converted this past Sunday morning. I'm sure glad they did.

Bowling Green, Kentucky: Mr. Davis, on Saturday morning while listening to your hymns on WLBJ I gave my heart to Christ.

Alexandria, Louisiana: Dear Governor Davis. I have

just had my 15th child and you have been so good to me I am naming him Jimmie Davis, Jr.

And finally, from *Quitman, Louisiana:* When they started this road work they moved our outhouse away. What are we going to do?

22. *Jimmie Davis—Storyteller!*

The author of this book has heard some of the best monologists, storytellers, stand-up comedians, and satirists in the business, from Las Vegas to New York, from NBC to CBS to ABC. Jimmie Davis is the best he's ever heard. The Davis style is impossible to impart on the written page; the way the man tells a story is as important as its content.

The Davis style is all "throw away." That is, the entire joke—or, as he calls it, "story"—is told in such a low-keyed manner that you might think the teller is inquiring about the time for someone's wake rather than going into a hilarious tale.

All of the Davis humor has one single element in common: all of it pokes fun at Jimmie Davis. Only a man with absolute confidence in himself and his talent could have such fun at his own expense.

So here are some Davis classics. They may make you laugh. That's what they've done to millions of people all across this land:

Jimmie explains his age this way. On one Saturday night in a city in Kentucky he and the Jimmie Davis Singers were to appear at the auditorium and then be present for the all day singing, preaching, and dinner on the ground the following day. Jimmie, Anna, and James Wilson were standing outside for some fresh air before going into the jam-packed auditorium for their part on the program. When up walked a tall, very thin Kentucky man, about 6–1, weighing about 115 lbs. and some fifty years of age.

"Jimmie, you've been in this business a long time haven't you?" I said a simple "yes." "And so has your wife, Anna?" Again I said "yes, she's a member of the Chuck Wagon Gang, started when she was fifteen years of age and they are still at it." A few moments later, just before we were to go into the auditorium, this man came by again. He said, "Jimmie, about how old are you now?" I said, "My friend, I don't mind telling you I lie about my age but just between us I'll tell you—I tell 'em I'm twenty-eight but really I'm twenty-nine". Then we rushed into the auditorium for our part in the program.

That man had a reserved seat right in the middle of the front row. I started off by saying, "I'm so glad to be back with you fine people and so glad you come out in such large numbers. (And just to go from one extreme to the other, I said I'd been in this business a long time.) I'll be ninety-four-years old in September, my wife (who has passed the fifty mark) is ten years older than I am and James Wilson (who is 35) is ten years older than she is, but we are in tolerable good health, thank the Lord."

The next day while we were eating dinner I was strug-

gling with a chicken leg. This same man walked up
again and says, "My Lord man, what do ya'll take to
stay in such good shape?" I said, "My friend we make a
tonic down at Peckerwood Hill." He said, "What kind of
hill? I said, "Peckerwood Hill. You can take a teaspoon
full of that stuff and can plow all day without going home
to lunch, never get hungry, and coon hunt all night long
and not be tired one bit. Now you can take a tablespoon
of this stuff and you can stay up three or four nights and
never get sleepy or tired. You can coon hunt, possum
hunt, climb trees and swing from limb to limb or go
dancing but I don't imagine you want to go dancing."
He said, "No, I cut out my sining a couple of years ago."

He said, "You got any of that stuff up here with you?"
I said, "No I don't because we want to get it fixed just
right for both man and beast before we put it on the
market."

"We had an old white-faced bull," I told him, "twenty-
nine years old, his head was dragging the ground, his
tail was dragging the ground, his eyes were kind of glassy
and he just about had it. We tied his head up to a fence
post and poured about a half pint of this tonic down him
and turned him loose. He curled his tail into a figure
eight, jumped out of the cow pen into the hog pen on
into the garden, and headed down the road to Newellton, Louisiana, which was seven miles away. He had to
pass three cattle farms. He stopped in each of these three
pastures along the way and made a social visit to at least
a half dozen cows on each farm and kept running and
bawling. We have one traffic light in Newellton and he
ran the red light and hit an old Model A Ford and
scattered it all over that part of town and kept going. We
haven't seen him since."

This Kentuckian said, "Man, I would like to have the

171

selling rights on that tonic in this county." I said, "You think you could sell it?" He said, "Sell it! I live out there in the old Antioch community and we'll get rich before we leave there. In fact, I don't have much money but I'm going to spend it all on that tonic. Well, I said give me your name and address and when we get it fixed like we want it, I'll contact you."

"I'll bet he's sitting on his front porch this morning waiting for a shipment of that tonic that's going to turn ole Antioch upside down.

I was one of eleven children, and, my friends, if you put eleven kids, mama, papa, grandpa, and grandma, two or three aunts, a few cousins, an old hound dog, and a cat with a bunch of kittens all in a two-room share-cropper's cabin in the red hills of north Louisiana on a hot August night, I'm telling you . . . you've had it!

I slept crosswise in a bed for so long—kids crawling in like new blind puppies, head first, feet first, finger in your eye, feet in your face, ice-cold feet in your back. You know, you couldn't tell if they were kicking you or kissing you.

We had the shortest covers in the world—both ways, length and width. There was always somebody falling out of bed or someone having nightmares and kicking you out. Besides that, there was always somebody wanting out. Now if he wants out, don't make the mistake of try-ing to keep him in there!

But once you get out of that bed and try to get back in, you have yourself a tough time, because they'll hold that cover like a bunch of cats and you'll run 'round and 'round that bed in your shirttail half of the night snatch-ing and grabbin' trying to get back in.

In fact, I didn't know you were supposed to sleep the

long way in bed until I got into the Governor's Mansion!

That day after the Inauguration ceremonies—meeting and greeting half the people in the state, eating hamburgers, hot dogs, gumbo, jambalaya, sweet milk, buttermilk, clabber, whey, blue john, and sassafras tea—I, along with everybody else, was ready to get a little rest.

We headed for the mansion, where I was going to have a room all to myself. Finally somebody said, "Well, it's bedtime." I said, "My friends, I'm ready!"

A man and a woman came to tuck me in for the night. Now I don't know whether you've ever been put to bed by a man and a woman—strangers! They led me up to that room. The man had on a frock tail coat that was dragging the floor, a big black bow tie that looked like buzzard's wings, and a starched collar that was so tight his tongue was sticking out. And that woman had on the longest dress I've ever seen. She walked around that bed three times and all that dress never did get in the room.

They started undressing me, and I figured that was just part of the program. Then they surprised, amazed, and astonished me when they pulled out a pair of the bluest striped pajamas you've ever seen in your life to put on me. These pajamas were silk, and I'd never been used to anything like that 'cause I was a gown man. And besides, that silk is something you've got to get used to! It's a long way from rags to silk.

When you put on silk pajamas for the first time, it'll tickle you to death and you're likely to run off and leave yourself. When they finally got me all buttoned up, I ran and jumped into the bed and slid all the way out into the hall. It looked like one of those old Charlie Chaplin movies.

They got me back in and straightened me out the long way, but when they left I put on my gown and I got crossways in that bed and got me a good night's sleep—the only good night's sleep I would have for the next four years!

You know, with that many people jammed in a little cabin, there's got to be something wrong with somebody all of the time. We had colds, croup, influenza, whooping cough, measles, red measles, German measles, and every other kind of measles. We had the rheumatism, gout, chicken pox, turkey pox, little pox, big pox, and the pox period!

We had another ailment out there—I can't think of what they call it now. All I know is they put sulphur and grease on it to cure it. Now you get somebody in that bed on a hot August night with a bad case of that stuff, way down in the middle of that bed with five or six kids riding him . . . you know there is such a thing as a human explosion. He's coming out of there!

We used to chase a lot of rabbits, and somebody was always having a big toenail knocked off, and Mama would put some of that sugar and turpentine with a little salve on the hurt toe and then wrap it with an old piece of bed sheet. She'd just keep wrapping and wrapping and get it all tied up so that it looked like a huge ear of corn sticking up. The hurt person would sleep on the side of the bed where he could hold that foot straight up to keep anybody from getting on it.

My friends, you can't hold that thing up all night!
You can't hold anything up all night long.

We had remedies out there that you've never heard of,

174

and I hope you never do. We had Grove's Chill Tonic, Cure All, turpentine, Cloverine Salve, and Rosebud Salve.

Now that Rosebud Salve was the sweetest smelling salve you've ever seen. You can put that stuff on you and go to church, and you won't offend anybody. Half of the folks will want to follow you home to try to find out what it is! They want some of it.

Most of the people in the community were great believers in poke berry root solution. They felt it would cure almost anything. I remember one time I had a rash, itching all over so bad I couldn't stand still. I didn't know what was the matter with me, and Mama didn't know either. So she cooked up a foot tub full of that poke root solution, and after supper, when it had cooled off, she got me out there in the backyard, stripped me off and dashed that stuff all over me. I literally caught on fire. I ran right through the cotton patch and the woods. They didn't find me until the next day at noon. When I got home I was well.

If we got the least bit congested, Mama got busy making a mustard plaster that she'd put on our chests to loosen them up.

One night she could tell I was taking a bad cold, coughing and snortin', and she was rambling around in the dark fixing that mustard plaster. We had run out of kerosene and didn't have a match in the house. She was feeling her way to the bed to put that hot mustard plaster on my chest, and she slapped it down. But she didn't hit my chest, and I nearly lost my mind!

Thought I was ruined. I headed out right through the cotton patch. I tore that little short nightgown into a thousand pieces.

My mama was strong on that asafetida, too, but you don't have to be strong on asafetida—asafetida'll take care of itself. They'd tie a string of that stuff around your neck, around your wrists, ankles—just anywhere you could find a place to tie it, they'd tie it on you. Sometimes Mama would tie one on me just to keep me from catching a disease from somebody. I'll guarantee you, if you haven't already got it, you're not going to get it because you won't be able to get close to anybody with that loud-smelling stuff on you!

I'll never forget the first date I ever had. There was an all-day singing and dinner on the grounds of the old Solemn Thought Church, and I was about fourteen-years-old. I met a girl who lived about eight miles away down the country, and she was the prettiest human being I had ever seen. I talked with her for a little while, and I didn't want to court—I wanted to get married!

I went to my father, who was standing at a table, and told him I'd found me a girl over there and I was going to get married. He said, "You're too young; nobody's going to marry you anyway." I told him, "I think so, because I was talking to that girl over by the tree, and she talked like she was about ready." He asked, "Do you mean that beautiful girl with the red dress?" I said, "Yes, that's the one." He said, "Son, you're not talking about a wedding. You're talking about suicide!"

I made a date with her to go see her the following Sunday. I had to walk about eight miles, but eight miles is no distance for a stepper when he's in love! Before I left the house, I tied a knot in my tie about the size of a soda-pop bottle and tied a string of that asafetida around my waist. I didn't think I was going to catch anything, but I not only wanted to look like something, I wanted to smell like something!

After pounding that dirt road for eight miles, I was sweating up a storm, and I walked into her house. The old man . . . the papa met me at the door, and he got one whiff of me in that asafetida and he took off. He circled the house about twice and wound up on top of the chicken house. Looked like an ostrich sitting up there!

Then, in came mama. She got a whiff and didn't say a word. She grabbed up about three dresses as she went by, and she looked like she was gone for good.

The girl came in—what I thought was my bride to be. She looked me straight in the face, but she didn't say one word. The room was pretty well fumigated by this time, and I could tell she was stifled. She snorted about twice before she took out. Gone!

There was nothing left but a five-month-old baby on the pallet. He got up and walked out of the room holding his nose with one hand and waving "bye-bye" with the other.

And there I sat, all alone by myself for thirty minutes. I didn't hear the sound of another human being. You know, you can't court by yourself. It takes two to tango, so I got up and headed for home.

I didn't see that girl again until about two years ago. I was down in Lubbock, Texas, on business, and I met this "bride-to-be" coming down the street.

She said, "Is that you?" I said, "Oh, yes, I'm the one." She said, "I want to ask you something that I've got a right to know, and that's all I'll have to say: What kind of perfume were you wearing that day?" I said, "Did you like that?" "Like it?" she replied. "I haven't seen my folks since. Nobody knows where anybody is."

177

Naturally, we didn't have much, which didn't bother us because no one had anything. We had no conveniences. Not only did we not have electricity and plumbing, we didn't even have an outhouse!

But we almost had one.

One year we sold a few chickens and a sow and pigs and got enough money to buy lumber to build an outhouse. We decided before launching such a project as this that we'd better find out exactly what we were building, because we'd never seen one.

We heard about a man named Smith who lived near Vernon, Louisiana, a small community about eight miles north of us, who actually had one. So Mama, Papa, and all eleven kids got into the wagon one morning and went up there to see this thing.

We looked it over pretty carefully and would have drawn a picture of it, but we didn't have a pencil. We had dinner with Mr. Smith, the proud owner of this unique structure. Smith mentioned that he had just made a lot of sugar cane syrup and Papa offered to trade a few pigs for thirty gallons of the syrup. Smith agreed and we loaded the cans onto the wagon and set out for home.

We were soon traveling down a seldom used road. It wasn't concrete, it wasn't blacktop, and it wasn't gravel. Just a plain old dirt road with thick limbs on either side practically covering it over. One of our mules rubbed against a wasp nest hanging on the end of a limb and in seconds wasps covered the two mules who took off with Papa trying unsuccessfully to hold them back.

There we were, eleven kids sitting in a wagon bed with thirty gallons of syrup flying every which way! The road was so rough and the mules were running so fast the lids to the syrup cans begin to come off and fly about like butterflies.

178

The syrup was soon spilling from all thirty buckets and the floor of the wagon was covered. We were slipping and sliding from one end to the other. Some of us were on our stomachs, some on our backs. The baby was on his face and the syrup was two inches deep about him. Papa grabbed him by his diaper and held him up so he wouldn't drown.

The mules ran until they couldn't run any more. That was the messiest gang you've ever seen when we began to clean up at home.

Next morning we told mama, "Please don't put any syrup on the table."

Even to this day I eat my pancakes plain.

Most everybody in the neighborhood heard about our proposed construction, and they all came down and brought hammers and handsaws, and we all started cutting timber and nailing and putting a good homemade board shingle roof on it.

We started to build a three-holer, but we were afraid that that would make for too much conversation in there, so we settled for a two holer.

We were making rapid progress on this building, and the kids and the grownups started lining up a few feet away like track athletes waiting for the gun to go off.

Everybody wanted to be first!

When someone said, "It's finished," everybody made a mad scramble for the grand entrance. They were so crowded in there, there was hardly room to stand, much less sit down.

And then the free-for-all fight started. One of my little brothers was fighting without his pants on, and one of the neighbor's kids didn't have anything on at all. When the fight was over, the only thing left standing of that thing we had hoped so long to use was one twelve-inch plank with a diamond-shaped hole cut in it where we had hoped to watch for the mail carrier and the Watkins man.

So we just forgot it all, and everybody went home and lived like we had before.

Neil Thomas served as sheriff of Jackson Parish for twenty years. Before he was sheriff, he was a barber in A. C. Holly's barbership in Jonesboro.

Back in his barbering days, Neil had a man in his chair all lathered up for a shave when a sharp pain hit him in the stomach. Neil told his customer, "I'll be right back," and he headed straight across the street to the town's outhouse—a six-holer—that sat on top of a red hill near Scroggin's Drug Store.

About the time that Neil got comfortable, the Brooks Ford Motor Company was showing a new buyer how to drive this Model T Ford. The salesman demonstrated where the neutral clutch, the brake clutch, and the reverse clutch were. The buyer took his seat back of the wheel, and the salesman said, "Move over and let me show you how to back up this hill so you can turn around."

The buyer replied, "Car's mine, I paid you for it, and you don't have to show me anything else. I know which clutch to press down to go backwards up this hill, and here I go!"

He had it wide open, and he hit that reverse and kept it down going up the hill straight into the outhouse, which he hit and scattered all over, with Neil Thomas right in the middle of it. Neil hit the ground running straight back to the barbershop.

The irritated customer in the chair said, "I'm ready for my shave now," but Neil said, "I can't shave you; someone else take care of him. I'm too nervous."

180

Neil went down the street and had a big sign painted, which he placed over the demolished outhouse. Here's how it read:

BE YE ALSO READY

FOR YE KNOWETH NOT

THE DAY OR THE HOUR

THE TRUCK COMETH.

Then Neil bought three boxes of Cloverine Salve and went home to bed.

This is a story Jimmie swears is true. The author has even heard others attest to its accuracy:

In Quitman (population about seventy-five) we didn't have an actual barbershop, but we had a small feed store that had been converted into one. The barber was Hardy "Churn" Brooks, who lived three miles out in the country on a dirt road at the Brooks Chapel Community. Hardy drove back and forth to work in a one-horse buggy, the round trip taking about an hour and a half.

One Thursday, I happened to be in town talking to Hardy when he said he'd forgotten something at home and would have to go and get it. I said, "I'll watch the shop for you." Hardy said, "That'll be fine. Nobody will be in today, they don't usually come in until Saturday." Then he hopped into his buggy and was on his way.

He hadn't been gone ten minutes when a long tall boy about nineteen years old came in from Choctaw Creek. He said, "Barber, I want to get a haircut." I said, "Have a seat." Then I asked him, "Any special kind of haircut you want?" He said, "Yes, I guess so. I'm getting married Saturday night." "Well," I replied, "you're in the right place, because I've got what we call a wedding special."

Now not only had I never given a haircut in my life—I'd never even tried it. But he sat down, and I put the cloth around his neck. I grabbed up a pair of manually operated clippers and started to work on him. I got to going high above his ears and the back of his head, and I tried to even it up all around, but all I was doing was going higher and higher. And it was too late to stop!

I backed off and took a look at it, and all the hair he had left on his head was a little patch about the size of a saucer.

I said, "Well, I think now what I'd better do is give you a shampoo." He said, "What's that?" I replied, "Your head's got to be clean when you walk down the aisle with your bride."

I got his hair washed and dried out good, and then I said, "What you need now is a good tonic." He blinked and said, "I may not need it, because I've been taking that Grove's Tasteless Chill Tonic for a week."

I replied, "This is altogether different. When you get this on, they'll know you've arrived."

I combed his hair, and he had so little left I didn't know where to part it, so I split it right down the middle. I said, "Now to cap it all off, you need a good singe job." He asked, "Lordy, what's that?" I said, "Let me show you."

I lit up a single match which was the size of a pencil and about ten inches long. He asked, "What does that do for me?" I said, "We singe the edge of your hair, and it keeps the good qualities in with all that sweet smell. Nothing can get in, and nothing can get out."

Finally I finished, removed the cloth, and said, "That's it." He asked, "How much do I owe you?" I said, "Nothing, wedding haircuts are free. In fact, we cut your hair free for two years."

He didn't know me and I didn't know him and I didn't want him to know me! He ran out of there and straddled that horse heading for home, the back of his head shining like a new moon.

I didn't think I'd ever see him again, but I was in town about six weeks later, and I saw him walking out of Sam Thomas' store. I went the other direction as quick as I could.

On Christmas Eve day I was in town, and before I knew it we saw each other face to face. He said, "Hello, barber." I said, "Howdy, my friend. You're looking fine. How was the wedding?"

He said, "We didn't have the wedding. I went to her house and she got a good look at me and the wedding was off. I guess she didn't believe in up-to-date haircuts."

I said, "Well, if she was that particular about it, maybe it's a good thing you didn't get married."

He said, "Yes, I think so, too, and I want to tell you, barber, you did me the biggest favor I ever received, because it helped me find out how childish and peculiar she was!"

In a community like Beech Springs where you're so far removed from doctors, somebody has got to do the doctor's job. My father lanced boils and carbuncles, sewed up wounds and pulled teeth.

Papa had a pair of forceps made by his father in a blacksmith shop and many are the times people came to get a tooth or five or six teeth pulled at the same sitting.

I remember one time, I was home from college between semesters, when a woman brought her fourteen-year-old daughter to our house to get a tooth pulled. She was very thin and her jaw was swollen like she had a baseball in her mouth. When Papa came out on the front porch with those forceps in his hand, she looked at him and said, "Oh no, I want Jimmie to pull it."

My Papa called me off to the side and asked, "Jimmie, did you ever pull a tooth?" I said, "No, but it looks like I'm about to go into the dentistry profession right here." Papa said, "You can pull it if you want to, but remember, that a tooth is much harder to pull than you think. The first thing you do is get these forceps as far down on the tooth in the gums as you can go. Then squeeze with all your might and twist a little as you pull. Don't twist too much or you'll break the tooth off. Don't worry about what the girl says or does because she's going to start fighting you like a settin' hen."

Well, the girl opened her mouth and I got hold of the tooth and when I rared back, she jumped up and locked her legs around my waist and started pounding me in the face. We left the porch and were heading toward the cowpen. Just as we reached the cowpen gate the girl went one way while the tooth, the forceps, and I went the other.

Papa examined the patient's mouth and motioned me to step over to the side where he whispered, "Son, don't know how to tell you this but you pulled the wrong tooth. Whatever you do, don't study dentistry!"

Then we had the Watkins man. My, what a man! He would come through the country in a one-horse wagon— a car couldn't travel those roads—about once a month and visit all those homes.

His wagon was full of merchandise, liniments, salves, tonics, food flavoring, spices, and most anything else you would want.

We'd always buy some of that Watkins Liniment. We'd

184

take some and rub some on. We'd get a jar of that Watkins ointment that was hotter than any pepper you've ever seen.

Now you've got to watch that stuff and be careful how you handle it and where you put it, because you're liable to run off and leave a good pair of pants! There was nobody we were happier to see than the Watkins man, unless it was Santa Claus!

Jimmie Davis recalls that when he was about nine years old he had the greatest Christmas he's ever had in his life.

I got a skinned blackbird and a hog bladder. We ate the blackbird and blew up that other thing. You've never seen such ball playing in all your days! Not even in the Superbowl.

With this tightly blown up bladder we played football, basketball, volleyball, townball, and baseball. We got very attached to this thing and took turns sleeping with it every night.

When it came to my four-year-old brother's turn he went to sleep holding it tightly in his arms. At about three o'clock in the morning he cried out "Mama! Mama! I've lost my bladder!" She got up and found it at the foot of the bed and put it back in his arms, and once again he was on his way to dreamland.

There was a stray cat about the place who ate our little chickens and ducks. We called her Suzie. Suzie very seldom struck a trot unless she was after a chick. But Suzie didn't know how fast she could trot and how far and how fast she could go.

We put some dry speckled peas in the dry hog bladder and backed that chicken-eating Suzie up to the fireplace and tied the hog bladder to Suzie's tail and opened the door. Away Suzie did go! Over the hills, over the hedges, and even over some of the small trees.

The last time we ever heard of Suzie or the hog bladder was from my uncle who lived at Punkin Center, between Hodge and Quitman. He said, "You know, I saw something, at least I thought I saw something yesterday that looked like a cat but it was too long for a cat, jumping too high for a cat, screaming too loud for a cat and such a tail as you've never seen! It might have been going to the hospital to have that wart removed from that tail. I hope she made it because that cat sure had a problem!"

Suddenly Davis' face grows soft; a dreamy quality washes over his eyes. The funny stories die on his lips so quickly you're not even certain that you heard them. His already musical voice grows more musical. And now he is trying to put into words what man has always had a need to tell—a yesterday that time has made kinder:

"But in the midst of all these wonderful and unusual experiences, with all the memories of my family together surrounded by the most wonderful neighbors in the world, it all comes back to me as memories of gold and treasures unspeakable.

"I never go into that section of Louisiana or anywhere near it, but what I go there—sometimes only for a moment—and recall all those memories and all those experiences.

"I was up there a short time ago, and as I walked across the lawn and into the yard and around that old house, I guess there were ten thousand bits of yesterday staring me in the face.

"I wish once again that I could relive those moments

spent with family and neighbors—those moments that meant so much to me.

"When I'm there I can always picture my mother standing in the back door about dusk and calling out, 'Children, come on home. It's suppertime.' "

J.W. + Dot Blankenship
3152 Turkey Mtn. R.d. n.E.
Rome, Ga. 30161   295-4198